A MILLION MILES WITH JESUS

Martha Olawale

Made in the USA

After God Heart Inc. USA

550 Congressional Blvd, STE 350, Carmel, Indiana, 46032

Websites: aftergodheart.org and abidingchristian.com

FOREWORD

A million miles... how many steps would that require?

It is exhausting to merely think of such a number! One pastor said that our discipleship journey is one in which the steps should be celebrated. That would be one long celebration, and rightfully so.

We were created for community. The most important person in our community is Jesus. The journey would be painful and fruitless without him. Well into my sixth decade of vocational ministry, my journey would have been very lonely and much more strenuous without the presence of great relationships, beginning with Jesus. "Presence" is one of the most vital attributes of the Divine Person of Jesus. He looked the woman at the well in the eye, He took the lame man by the hand and met personally with a religious leader under cover of darkness.

Other people are very important as well. Look up the expression "one another" or variations of it in Paul's writings, especially the relationships he mentions in Romans 16, and you will see the importance he placed on true community.

There is an African proverb that I heard years ago, and I have learned and experienced its truth: *"If you want to go fast, go alone; If you want to go far, go together."*

Martha has tapped into many timeless truths on her journey, and she so eloquently shares them with us. This book can become a timeless treasure to its readers if we view it as a virtual mentor. As she bares her soul and shares her life experiences, we should use her many examples to encourage us on our own journey of "<u>A Million Miles with Jesus</u>."

As I watched David and Martha navigate a very challenging season in their lives – he was matriculating at Florida State University, earning his doctorate – there was never a time when I did not see the fruit of the Spirit demonstrated in and through their lives. They were always a joy to be around – there IS joy in the journey, even in difficult seasons. People who know them know that they are encouragers, and everyone needs to be encouraged! It was my privilege to be their pastor and friend during part of that season of their lives. I grew in grace because of them.

Martha takes the experiences of a daughter, wife, mother, and friend, and provides practical advice for our journey. Her experiences are unique to her, but they are not uncommon to us as we walk with Jesus. There are many Godly women in the Bible who filled significant roles in the advancing of the Kingdom and provided tremendous examples for us. Martha is a present-day model of such women.

She puts me in mind of this Scripture: *"So, my child, draw your strength from the grace that is in Christ Jesus. Take the things you heard me say in front of many witnesses and pass them on to faithful people who are also capable of teaching others."* 2 Timothy 2:1-2 (Common English Bible – CEB)

This book points us to that grace which provides strength. As we "hear" her testimonies, we would all be wise to pass them on to faithful people.

Ron McCants

Director of Life Principles Training

Global Outreach Department

In Touch Ministries

Atlanta, USA

TABLE OF CONTENTS

PREFACE

I picked up my first pen to write a Christian article when I was fifteen. Since then, I have found comfort in expressing anything God lays in my heart through writing. As a teenager, I had a writing notebook everywhere, whether at Church, School, or on our home's balcony. It even determined my career choice. While worship is my first love, and I served in that capacity for most of my Christian life, writing is a crucial part of God's call over my life, and the abidingchristian.com website is in response to that.

Through the years and experiences, I have realized that if God wants to say something through you until you say it, rest will elude you. The Abiding Christian blog is a response to a nudge in my heart to write what I am learning at the foot of the cross as I walk this rough road through life. Each article is from a heart longing to honor Christ and to see Him honored by other Christians. Most of them were impressed in my heart as I lay awake in the middle of the night with everything around me quiet, and all I could hear was the whizzing sound of my sleeping husband beside me.

At first, I wondered where the words would come from and where I would get the topics to write about each week. It has been over four years since then, and although I had a rough start, the Holy Spirit has guided my heart and hands to publish consistently each week. I am growing in trust, obedience, and strength from my time with God and sitting with a great community of friends.

The articles are non-sequential, written independently at different times and seasons of reflection. They are compilations of the first two years' articles of Abiding Christian. Some of them were written during the COVID-19 crisis. I shared the weight of that season of uncertainty with the world then, but my resolve was anchored in walking with God. No matter where you are in your journey with Christ, you will find a nugget or two as you read.

Walking with Jesus means that sometimes you feel like running around in a park full of roses, but it also feels like crawling through the mud at a boot camp when life's cares cloud the view of Heaven. Regardless, the joy and fulfillment that come with our salvation are unmatchable, and the hope of eternity with Jesus trumps every discomfort we face. As you read, I pray that God meets you right where you are and shines the torch of Heaven on your heart to receive what He intends for you.

DEDICATION

I I love Rebecca Aderibigbe, my late mother. You will meet her in some articles. I saw her live as every Christian should; she is my earthly Christ-like example. Mum did not fake it or chicken out of difficult situations but faced them all boldly in faith. She was Christian at home, at Church, on the streets, and at the neighbor's house. She prayed for the sick, fed the hungry, housed the homeless, and presented Christ to the lost. I am grateful to be called her daughter and privileged to have lived under the same roof as her.

ACKNOWLEDGMENT

I live with him if you are looking for where a man after God's heart lives. It's an honor to walk through life holding Seunmi's hands. He epitomizes "All in for Jesus or not in at all." He grounds me through his devotion to God and consistency in pursuing Him. I've seen David pray daily and study the Bible for twenty-five years. He is grumpy without daily time with God and can't function until he prays and reads the Bible. Every topic with him leads back to Jesus. His love for God is a catalyst for mine, and his leadership makes it conducive for me to thrive.

I love Seunmi and love loving him. He is my leader, hero, priest, encourager, best friend, mission manager, brother, and partner. Managing "Abiding Christian" would have been difficult, but for the amazing children God blessed me with. My creative evangelist Desayo, gentle leader Joseph, and wise, creative genius RonDaniel. I love you. I love your presence, and the sound of your voice drowns the noise in my world.

Thank you, Dad (Tandy Aderibigbe), for teaching me to walk with my head high as your daughter. Bishop David Oyedepo, thank you for showing me the liberating power of God's Word, igniting the Kingdom warrior in me. To all my Christian friends, from my years in Nigeria: Lagos, Ogun, and Yobe states to my years in the United States, Florida, and Indiana, thank you! I am also grateful for the Church of Christ and all my local churches. From my early Christian years at "Go Ye Church of God" to other churches in thirty-plus years: "Living Faith World Outreach," "Redeemed Christian Church of God," Christian Heritage Church," "City Church," and "Northview Church," thank you for providing sanity in a very complex world and for enriching my life through the years.

Being God's child is the bedrock of my identity, and I'm unapologetic about my love for Christianity and my brothers and sisters. Just put me with Christians, and I will be home. My Christian friends have made Heaven look closer through fellowship, time in worship, prayer, eating, laughing, crying, and sharing. I am grateful to God for sharing this path with them and keeping me focused on the kingdom.

My ultimate gratitude goes to my Heavenly Father, who has been constant at every turn, height, and depth of my existence—He, who, in His mercies, chose me to be a vessel in His hands. *"Now unto the King eternal, immortal, invisible, the only wise God, be honor and glory forever and ever. Amen." 1 Timothy 1:17.*

PART I

MY STORY IN HIS STORY

"Why do the nations conspire and the people plot in vain? The kings of the earth rise up, and the rulers band together against the Lord... The One enthroned in heaven laughs." Psalm 2:1-2,4a

Humanity continues to seek answers to its origin from any available source, ignoring the source who came down from Heaven to walk among us. The more we search, the less we know. We look to oceans for answers and find none; we look to the stars beyond our galaxies and find none. Our quest to disregard God's sovereignty leads us beyond where humanity can reach but reduces the understanding of our story in His story.

The story of God starts with God and unfolds in the past, present, and future of time. God is not a historical figure or a scientific discovery. He is neither a hero in a once-upon-a-time fable nor a character in our plot lines. God is our creator and is as majestic and present today as before the beginning of time.

The complexity of His existence speaks through a billion stars, and the depth of His love speaks through Christ's life, death, and resurrection. The world has welcomed, celebrated, and denounced many heroes who are now reduced to the pages of books. But God remains God, and the story of the baby in the manger remains the beginning of man's return to God's original intent to fellowship with mankind.

If the earth quivers or the universe unravels, God will still be God, and the blood of Christ will still speak louder than the blood of Abel. Humanity can call a round table meeting to denounce God's existence, but that won't reduce Him from His Sovereignty, and we can stomp a hole in the heart of the earth, but that will not reduce His glory either. We can keep trying to make sense of the story of our existence, but each dot of the lines we tread will always point back to God.

THE DEPTH I SEEK

"You will seek me and find me when you seek me with all your heart." Jeremiah 29:13

Waking up each morning throws us into a spinning circle of choices and a passion to make each second of the day count. We often thrust ourselves into a million activities and leave God on the back burner, locked in a corner. We live on a diet of intimacy with ourselves instead of with the Holy Spirit and dwelling in God's presence. We only peep into the little room we have created for God when we need Him but then shut the door on Him as soon as we feel we are up to the task.

As I grow in age and walk with God, I learn more about my limitations and that their presence does not define me; rather, they grow me. These limitations are simply the catalysts that thrust me deeper into my dependence on God. I am learning that my abilities are nothing but scraps from the abundance of grace embedded in my redemptive nature.

As my limitations call out, God's grace answers and reduces the mountain before me to rubble.

When we are resilient in pursuing God, we enjoy all He has freely given us through salvation despite the challenges. Our limitations will not deprive us but draw us closer to the heart and always-ready warm embrace of our Father. While deep calls to deep (Psalm 42:7), the treasures beyond the reef of self-reliance are worth every dig, and the unending road of adventures with Christ is worth treading.

I seek depth, a place designed by the statutes of Heaven where God is constant in my thoughts, actions, and reactions. A place where He is the rhythm in the note of my life song, and His heart is the source through which my mind pumps every drop of blood. I long for that depth that takes me beyond the shores of doubt and anxiety to ride on the waves of God's glory. I am a depth seeker, and the treasures I seek lie in Christ alone.

OF THE INCREASE OF HIS KINGDOM

"Of the increase of his government and peace, there shall be no end..." Isaiah 9:7a

I've had a series of reports about some people not wanting to be under the Lordship of God or identify as Christians. However, thinking that this reduces the effect of the work of redemption is relatively false as I see differently because I speak through the lens of God. While, like every generation, the battle for the hearts of humanity rages, millions are embracing the message of God's love yearly, and through them, what I see is the increase of His Kingdom.

Somehow, we flipped the script, mistaking the narrow road for the broad. There was never a suggestion in scripture that the broad gate leads to Heaven. Jesus said in Matthew 7:13b-14, *"For wide is the gate and broad is the road that leads to destruction, and many enter through it. But small is the gate and narrow the road that leads to life, and only a few find it."*

If we think about the significance of the essence of our faith and the power behind the force that has kept the story of the cross alive for thousands of years, we will approach evangelism with better resolve. It is not the acceptance of the multitude in one generation that authenticates the saving power of the cross; it is each soul saved year after year, generation after generation since Jesus paid the ultimate price for our sins. Twelve became one hundred and twenty and then multiplied into millions. Jesus lives through each salvation story, and herein lies our resolve.

To speak of the God who has defied time, the rise of kings, and the folding of kingdoms is the most incredible privilege anyone can have. Understanding this propels us to reach the world around us for Jesus, celebrating each soul's salvation like a million people saved from death. Christ remains immutable to change because He exists beyond the earth's foundations, and we are simply banner bearers of a truth that never ends.

Christianity is not dying because it cannot. There are millions of Christians in all nooks and corners of the world, and in each believer is a fire, no matter how small, ignited by their new birth in Christ, and that fire will always give birth to more fires. Each day, even in the most unlikely places, many people still stream in surrender to the foot of that rugged cross at Calvary.

The story of the crucified and resurrected Christ did not give birth to a religion; it simply introduces us to the love of God. And from one generation to another, that love story keeps capturing the hearts of people, young, old, poor, and rich, from different creeds and languages across the globe. Imagine what the devil thought when he saw Jesus take His last breath on the cross. It looked like the end because he had no idea it was the beginning of the redemptive story of man's return to his maker. No matter how much humanity tries, we cannot write Christ out of His story because our history and future are wrapped up in a fraction of who He is.

WHAT IS GOOD AND WHAT IS NOT

"God saw all that he had made, and it was very good." Genesis 1:31

"When the woman saw that the fruit of the tree was good..." Genesis 3:6

It feels good to gulp a bottle of cold, sweet soda on a hot summer day instead of drinking flat-tasting water. We can throw caution into the wind at the moment because all that matters is that it quenches your thirst and satisfies your throat. However, the consequence and price of doing so might cost more than the first gulp's satisfaction because of the effect of the content on your health. The story of creation introduces us to the human gravitation toward momentary pleasure in place of long-term consequences.

If we think about the intricacies of being human and how we know how to live and navigate a complex world; eat, sit, walk, rest, sleep, talk, cry, and dance, we'll agree that buried within us is the nature of God and the power of the knowledge of good and evil. The entirety of our world hangs on the balance of this truth, which tilts to either side in all situations. Our soul responds to how we have nurtured it; when it is godly, it will always embrace good as defined by the life of Jesus.

I have been asked, "How do you know?" How do you know God exists? Why do you believe Jesus is Lord? How do you know you will go to Heaven when you die? How do you know there is Heaven? How do you know what is good and what is not? These questions are wrapped up in a simple language you do not need anyone to interpret; take a moment to allow your redeemed soul to answer them because it speaks the dialect of Heaven. Trust me, a soul surrendered to Jesus knows its maker's voice and can decipher what is good and what is evil.

God made man in His likeness and made us co-creators in a universe created by Him, and with privilege comes responsibilities and consequences. A simple inclination that God is anything but good goes against His core attribute and the person of Jesus. God's definition of good is whole, while man's definition of good is fragmented and relative. God is always good, regardless of our shortsightedness and uncertainties, and how we see it does not reduce His wholesomeness. He entered a formless, dark, empty world and brought light and order. He called the things that were not into existence (Romans 4:17). It is as simple as what is good is God, and what is not good is not God, but it takes a heart surrendered to Jesus to understand this truth.

THE WARRIOR IN YOU

*"What, then, shall we say in response to these things?
If God is for us, who can be against us?... No, in all
these things, we are more than conquerors through
him who loved us." Romans 8:31,37*

Every morning, I wake up to another heart-pricking news. The world is spinning in all directions, aside from God's. There's always an event that calls me to raise my head to Heaven and lower my knees to the ground. Before the brokenness of yesterday is mended, I see another crack today, and my spirit breaks with it. My soul tells me God can fix these because He sent me here as an extension of Heaven, and as a soldier of the cross, I fight until my last breath.

As Christians, do we get to cower in a corner, or do we join Heaven's call to stand ready to go when Christ commands? We are infused with the blood of the Lamb and direct descendants of the Lion of Judah, and we should live our lives in a way that reflects that identity. If I don't do my part, I will deny the world the grace God has mercifully bestowed on me to show the world how much He loves them.

In a world where everyone has a victim status hanging on their identity, our Christian faith should be the distinguishing factor. There is a warrior in you, a spirit ignited by the redemptive power of the Lord Jesus Christ. Although the battle rages on, *"In all these things, we are more than conquerors through Him who loved us."*

God is not fighting against humanity; He is fighting for humanity. There is a roar from Heaven, calling the soldiers of the cross to raise their banner of righteousness and fight the good fight of faith. Change your stance and join the battle to lead the world around you to the foot of the cross. Dust off your horn, prepare to echo the call to salvation, and fight for those still ignorant of God's love. You are children of Zion and have Heaven's backing; live that reality.

WHEN YOU KNOW GOD

"The king said to Daniel, "May your God, whom you serve continually, rescue you!" Daniel 6:16b: "If it is so, our God whom we serve is able to deliver us from the burning fiery furnace, and he will deliver us out of thine hand, O king." Daniel 3:17

The resilience in the Christian faith is born out of a deep-seated confidence in God, a resolute that is immovable by circumstances or geography. Why else will the martyrs choose to lay their lives down in place of a man's defined "Freedom" that denies the power of the cross and the Lordship of Christ?

It's not where we are or what we are going through that defines God; it's who and all He is that defines Him. God is who He says He is, and our belief, or the lack of it, cannot change that.

God is not an elusive sky being. He is a present, consistent Father. I know God because I have experienced His presence in the most challenging seasons of my life and enjoyed the most beautiful dance around my world with Him. He is that friend that never leaves yet never loses His welcome. Each morning with Christ brings a newness of strength and vigor to my life, and He is the reason my world has meaning.

I have walked through several stressful roads where no one else can tread with me, where I felt my heart would give way and my world would come crumbling down before my eyes. While the world around me keeps moving on, in those moments, God stays consistent and holds me through the days and nights. I know God because I have seen Him steadfast in seasons that push my humanity to the brim of the cliff.

As a child of God, if you have ever been pushed against a wall and found yourself breaking through it, you know God is not defined by our circumstances nor bows to it. If you have been overwhelmed by exhaustion because of situations within and beyond your control and somehow end up on the winning side, then you know God never fails. If you have enjoyed the peace that passes all understanding and feel swaddled by a hand you cannot see, then you know that even if all you have is taken from you, God is always enough.

There are no tides high enough to drown the calming presence of God or darkness so thick that it can overcome

His glory. It took knowing God for Daniel, Shadrach, Meshach, and Abednego to defile a king's decree to honor the King of kings. There is so much more to knowing God that all the pressure in the world cannot pull you away once you have experienced Him.

IN THE BEGINNING, GOD!

"In the beginning, God created the Heavens and the earth. Now the earth was formless and empty, darkness was over the surface of the deep, and the Spirit of God was hovering over the waters." Genesis 1:1-2

I had a conversation about the first verse of Genesis with a group of friends over two decades ago, and I still remember how it got us fired up. Even today, when I think about those first four words of the Bible, I shiver at the wholesomeness of God. That verse stirs something inside my soul, leading me to bow to my God and King. The perfect combination of words put me in my place and God where He belongs. It reminds me that before I was, He was. Before the oceans were, He was before the stars were, He was, and He alone crowns the entire universe with His glory.

God existed before the beginning of time and before the first existence. Think about it: the things that have taken humanity generations to know and marvel at—science, innovation, and all the discoveries He is unveiling to us— are just minute details of His Majesty. He knew everything before the earth was formed and ruled over it all.

There was none before God, and He reigns from the beginning of one galaxy to the end of another. He is the Alpha, the Omega, the beginning, and the end. Regardless of what I think of God and how far and wide my mind tries to understand Him, He is more significant, remarkable, and mightier than human comprehension.

Speaking of the greatness of God, David said in Psalm 24:1-2," *The earth is the Lord's, and the fullness thereof; the world, and they that dwell therein. For He hath founded it upon the seas and established it upon the floods. "* God took what was nothing and made something out of it. By speaking, He shaped the earth, dividing the waters from the waters and the daylight from the night light.

"In the beginning" started with GOD, and although He gave humanity authority over His creation, we are not compared to who He is. I tremble at the glorious power of the Most High, for He is God and will always be God. I join the trillion stars and galaxies to stand in awe of my maker, and while my little mind can never fathom the depth and height of Him, every fiber of my being worships His majesty.

WHERE GOD LEADS

"The Lord had said to Abram, "Go from your country, your people, and your father's household to the land I will show you." Genesis 12:1

Imagine what the outcome of Abram's disobedience would have been. When God told Him to leave his home and family and head to a destination he had never been to, he had the choice to stay or obey the voice of God. He chose to obey, and due to his obedience, he got a new name and opened the door to impacting many generations after him. Through trust, he lived up to what God said in Genesis 17:5: *"No longer will you be called Abram; your name will be Abraham, for I have made you a father of many nations."*

I have tried to guide God many times instead of following His leadings; the outcome is never pleasing. My human brain draws the map based on my understanding, leaving out God's will on each road I have paved for myself instead of allowing Him to lead me on my journey. While He has been faithful, even in my wrong turns, I have only known satisfaction when walking on the steps He lays. Now I know that if I walk through the fire according to God's leading, I will be just fine, and if I stand on the mountaintop or lie in the valley below according to His leading, I am safe.

His leading may come with some discomfort and uncertainty, but where He leads, there will always be peace. Like Abram, when God calls us out of our comfort zone, His presence will guide us to a destiny that will outlive us. Today, as Christians, we still regard ourselves as descendants of "Father Abraham," just as God promised him because He obeyed.

Destinies are resting on your obedience and broken places waiting to be mended, so trust God and allow Him to enlarge your coast. God's perfect will is where He wants you to be. If you do not stay or go where God wants you to, you cannot do all God wants you to do or positively affect the lives He wants you to impact. While God's presence will follow us to the darkest ends, His perfect will for us is where He wants us to be, and in that lies our absolute satisfaction.

MEETING "ME"

"For you created my inmost being; you knit me together in my mother's womb. I praise you because I am fearfully and wonderfully made; your works are wonderful, I know that full well." Psalm 139:13-14

I had no say in the family I was born into, and that singular fact shaped many factors that got me where I am today. I did not get to choose the color of my skin, the texture of my hair, or the color of my eyes. They are all part of the package that makes up my physical attributes. However, these things do not define me.

In a world where everyone builds a box to put "Me" in — the box of race, affluence, gender, fame, geography, marriage, motherhood, church denomination, etc., I must define "Me" through the eyes of my creator. I am more than a woman, daughter, wife, mother, etc. The only name that fits me is whom God called me — the daughter of the Most High.

25

There are so many layers to the mountain of complexities that sum up my life—layers unraveled by seasons of pain, moments of happiness, bright colors, and gray areas. There is simply no way any human or single factor can define me. I am born out of Christ's sacrifice on the cross and live my life through the working grace of the Holy Spirit.

The struggles and confusion that ensue in the quest to "Find yourself" stem from a place of confusion that cannot be soothed until you find your way to the foot of the cross. Paul writes in Galatians 2:20, *"I have been crucified with Christ, and I no longer live, but Christ lives in me. The life I now live in the body, I live by faith in the Son of God, who loved me and gave himself for me."* As Christians, we live in the reality of who we truly are because we are completed through salvation.

I met "Me" the day I met Jesus and found my identity at the foot of the cross. At Calvary, I saw myself through the eyes of a loving Father who continually delights in me. I am no longer bound by the chains that held me captive to my sins, leaving me wandering like a lost child because God's grace is sufficient for me. You can push, pull, and shove me; I will always land in the safe hands of Jesus.

MIND YOUR MIND

"A good man brings good things out of the good stored up in his heart, and an evil man brings evil things out of the evil stored up in his heart. For the mouth speaks what the heart is full of." Luke 6:45

I recently heard a song I had not heard in decades and was surprised to remember every lyric. The simple trigger was a melody that sounded familiar from a time I could only travel to in my dreams. I had never thought about it for years, but those words were buried deep in my mind without my knowledge.

Unless we live alone on an island, we cannot control most things we see or hear, but understanding our mind's power helps us better navigate our environment. Solomon said in Proverbs 4:23, *"Above all else, guard your heart, for everything you do flows from it."* With all the noise we must deal with and the wealth of information available today, intentional assimilation is necessary to stay afloat in the drowning ocean.

I always tell my children, "What you devote your mind to forms what you believe." No matter how bizarre a school of thought or a thing is, when you hear it consistently, it determines your interpretation. And what you stand and fight for reflects the well from which your mind draws. The mind is not an idle part of our being; it is the most active and potent. It absorbs and controls our actions and reactions; no matter how intelligent a person is, the mind rules.

The human mind is like a well deeper than the ends of the ocean, and it is important to be conscious of what we pour into it. A little here and a little there fill the bucket we draw from it. If you fill your mind with goodness, you will draw goodness from it; when you fill it with filth, you will draw dirt from it. You might not always have power over the information you are exposed to, but when it is within your power to change the frequency you subscribe to, consciously consider the health of your mind.

As Christians, our foundation is built on the life and death of Christ Jesus, and the bounty of our hearts should reflect this truth. If all the world can see are things other than goodness, mercy, and grace when they tug at us to respond, then we are missing the mark. There may be many pollutants around us, but our minds should be so saturated with the beauty and joy of walking with God that they subconsciously reject things that do not honor Him.

I CAN'T, GOD CAN

"Casting down imaginations, and every high thing that exalts itself against the knowledge of God and bringing into captivity every thought to the obedience of Christ." 2 Corinthians 10:5

My husband and I spent ample time living the graduate student life: little money, lots of books, and sleepless nights. With the demand and years required to obtain a Ph.D., one will think the knowledge gained through the process is comprehensive. However, my husband once explained that it means becoming an expert in a specific area of knowledge for a particular period.

According to him, having a doctorate in engineering does not mean you know everything about engineering; it only means you know a lot about a little. The knowledge you gain through the process is tied to your area of focus. Certainly, he said, "If you do not continue to build on what you have learned, your gained knowledge will become obsolete."

The most revolutionary theories have been improved or debunked, and no human can claim to know it all because there is always something we lack knowledge of. Even the most brilliant man in the room fails at some point. And no matter how widely read or traveled we are, we can never cover all knowledge across space and time because our brains can only assimilate so much. We are limited by how far we can absorb and process knowledge, and our humanity bows to the universe's vastness, history, and future.

I was typing "I can do all things through Christ" on my phone, and the moment I wrote "I can do all things," the device auto-filled my sentence with "by myself." Our haughty hearts have created a charade that our human abilities reduce God's majesty. The belief system that argues that, somehow, we know better than God is not just false but unwise. In His graciousness, God releases knowledge to man in bits and pieces so we can grasp a little more of His unsearchable greatness.

Even when humanity can make a home beyond the skies and figure out how to live beneath the ocean, the unknown will always limit what we know. Regardless of the knowledge we gain, the complexity and limitations of our humanity will always unravel in the face of adversities. And no matter how we have charged ourselves into believing in the power of positive thinking, we crumble under the weight of forces beyond our control. We might be proficient in one thing and clueless about a million other things, but God is all-knowing.

Accepting our humanity and bowing to God's sovereignty dispels our fear of failing. A surrendered heart is a constant reminder that although we are limited, God is unlimited; though our humanity is finite, God's divinity is infinite; we are mortal, and He is immortal. The strongest and wisest of us have "Can'ts," but God does not. Bringing our thoughts in subjection to honor God dismisses our struggles with making sense of life. Until we realize that only God can, we will live as slaves to the "Can'ts" we face in life and break our backs under the burden of trying to fix things only God can fix.

WALK WITH ME

"But Ruth replied, "Don't urge me to leave you or to turn back from you. Where you go, I will go, and where you stay, I will stay. Your people will be my people, and your God my God." Ruth 1:16

The role of a mother is crucial in the life of her children. How she handles situations and responds to the world around her affects the way her children will act when they grow up. I was privileged to have had a mother who loved God and fought like a warrior for the lives of her children and the people God brought her way. She loved without boundaries and governed her home with strength. When you look into her eyes, you will see the kindness that overcomes any form of shame coupled with strength that takes on giants.

I have been searching the internet for information on how to say "My daughter in Spanish" recently. Among the top searches before I could type "…in Spanish" was "My daughter hates me." When I saw that, I stopped typing because it grieved my heart. How can a relationship that should be one of the most treasured be tainted with the word "hate?" It was so unexpected that it affected my mood the entire day. I was sad to realize how far the world has deteriorated to the point that something so special is corrupted because we are losing our grip on our strengths as women.

Some of the world's most outstanding leaders, athletes, scientists, and preachers have mothers who championed values that formed the bedrock upon which they built their careers. A mother-daughter/mother-son relationship is a gift from God and should be approached intentionally. The power we have as women in shaping our world begins with who we walk with and how we lead behind the walls of our homes. When Christ paves our path, it will be easy to guide through the eyes of a Father who loved mankind enough to die for an underserved world.

I treasure the kindness, grace, and wisdom my mother sprinkled along the way as I now journey through the path that she walked. Against what the world would have us believe, within mothers lies the spirit of excellence to equip the next generation to impact the world with positivity and brilliance through godly examples. Whatever role God calls us to play within and outside our homes when we walk with Jesus, we can run a million miles.

SPOT THE DIFFERENCE

"...pursue righteousness, godliness, faith, love, endurance and gentleness. Fight the good fight of faith..." 1 Timothy 6:11-12

As a teen, one of my favorite games was "Spot the Difference." I love the intrigue of spotting each hidden difference in the pictures. It is a puzzle in two pictures, and it engages most of your human senses, giving an exciting sense of accomplishment when you are done. At first glance, both pictures in the game look exactly the same, and it is not until you divide each of them into sections and look closer that you realize a few things have been altered to make them unnoticeably different.

This game recently got me thinking, and the thoughts were not as intriguing and fun. Rather, it was a sober reflection of my life as a Christian living in a world that conflicts with my beliefs. I imagined my life as a believer in a picture placed beside the life of someone without the knowledge of who Jesus is. How different is my life? Will others have to squint and spend hours trying to figure out differences between my values, my attitude to life, my love for people saved and unsaved, my approach and acceptance of culture and its emergence? Or will they immediately look at both pictures and note undeniable differences?

As we follow our shepherd and big brother, the Lord Jesus, our life should reflect who He is. Though He was a man, He was different when He walked the earth. He loved differently, He looked different, He talked differently, and everyone who encountered Him knew it. Salvation is transforming—through it, our lives should look more and more like Christ. Romans 8:29 says, *"For those He foreknew, He also predestined to be conformed to the image of His Son that He might become the firstborn of many brothers and sisters"* (KJV).

Jesus did not just blend in with the crowd. He was undeniably different, even from those who claimed to know the laws. The kingdom of God was His mission and message; He taught it, lived it, and left footprints on the sands of His life on earth for us to follow. In the teachings of Christ, there was a clear distinction between the Kingdom of God and the world. The culture taught justice; He taught justification. The culture said, "Stone her," He said, "Forgive her." The culture ostracized; He healed. Our lives should speak volumes about the nature of the kingdom of God, where we now share citizenship with Christ through redemption. The book of Colossians talks about being *"translated from the*

Kingdom of darkness into the Kingdom of God's dear Son" (1:13).

It bothers me that the world seems confused and questions the moral standard of a Christian man or woman. They measure our sense of morality by the dictates of the culture and not by the scriptures.

There should be no debate regarding believers' stand on any issue or question. We live by the word of God. Our acceptable values should not "evolve" with an accepting culture but should be consistent with God's word.

"...but because ye are not of the world, but I have chosen you out of the world..." John 15:19

The "I am a Christian" declaration should answer any social or cultural question. Our stand should be firm and true to God's word. Christianity should not be reduced to church attendance and the names by which we go. It is far beyond that. It is living like Jesus. We reflect the person of Jesus Christ and are carriers of His divine grace to live *right* in a very dark and morally bankrupt world. Our values should not be easily bent by emerging culture. Christian values should shape culture, not vice versa. No matter where we live on earth, regardless of the culture we call home, the Bible should be our trusted compass to navigate through life. Christ paid a high price for our salvation. He became a man, suffered like a man, and was killed by a man. Philippians 2:8 says, *"...He humbled Himself and became obedient unto death, even the death on the cross!"* Though He is God, He lived in our world and suffered the ultimate shame to bring us redemption.

Just take a minute to reflect on your values and the things that are acceptable to you as a believer: How you love, how you talk, how you judge, and how you channel your fear. Do you fear man more than you fear God? Take another minute to think of Jesus standing in your place, surrounded by the many vices we face today. If you play a quick game of "Spot the Difference," will your values and life choices be more like Christ's, or will they be more in line with the culture of your time?

When you affirm your faith as a Christian, remember it is a declaration of your allegiance to Christ and your desire to live like Him. You are a reflection of Jesus, and you cannot lead people to Him if you do not look like Him. You are part of His plan to make the world a better place and shine forth the rays of righteousness in your little world.

"You are the Light of the world, a city that is set on a hill that cannot be hidden…… let your light shine before men, that they may see your good deeds and praise your father in heaven". Mathew 5:14, 16

QUIT COMPLAINING; GIVE GOD CONTROL

"Trust in the Lord with all your heart and lean not on your own understanding; in all your ways submit to him, and he will make your paths straight." Proverbs 3:5-6.

L etting go is difficult because we feel better in control and know the A to Z of life's puzzles. Even when we can't figure it out, we keep staring at it, hoping to work it out without God. We suppress the nudge to knock on Heaven's gate until we reach our wit's end.

The children of Israel, despite every effort by God to gain their trust, wavered over and over. They complained about eating the same food when the alternative was to go without. They complained about their deliverance from Egypt, though they suffered for over four hundred years in bondage under Pharaoh. They complained about water rushing too fast when the alternative was drought.

How often do we tell God, "If you answer this prayer, I will trust you forever?" However, our subsequent discomfort leads us to scramble over everything and cower in defeat. The fact that God delivered us from the missteps and troubles in the past does not count towards His faithfulness, and we search for alternatives outside of His grace. We are constantly guilty of gazing at the present worries instead of remembering God's faithfulness from yesterday.

Trust is fundamental in any relationship, especially in our walk with Christ. More than anyone else, He is patient and consistent in dealings with His children. Depending on God means releasing everything to Him in absolute trust, regardless of the terrain He will walk us through. Only trusting Him means He is our only life anchor with no alternative lifeboats.

In my short life, I have traveled some difficult roads but have enjoyed God's strength through them all. Sometimes, I look back and ask, "How did I get through that?" If we can trust that God is who He says He is: eternal, sovereign, almighty, good, and savior, we will enjoy rest even in the face of life's greatest struggles.

That we cannot see God face to face does not mean we should not trust Him more than reality permits us. Despite their knowledge and experience with the power of God, the children of Israel did not trust God any more than people who had not witnessed a single miracle. They even ventured to build a golden calf in place of the true God who delivered them from Egypt. The fact that He walked them through the sea was not enough to keep their eyes on God, and at the slightest opportunity, they sought alternatives.

We noticed that our daughter would whine because of one missing favorite snack, even when she had other choices. So, we deliberately skip buying it to teach her that even when you do not have your favorite, you are not worse without it. It is the same with our heavenly father. While He wants us to enjoy all that life can offer, He also wants us to grow in our faith in Him and empathy toward others.

When David said in Psalm 23:1, *"The Lord is my shepherd, I lack nothing,"* he was not referring to his riches or undefeatable army. He was talking about the sufficiency that comes from walking with God. He knew that with God on his side, even when he faced the Goliath of life, he was not alone.

When we allow God to oversee the affairs of our lives, we lack nothing because we enjoy the constant presence of the King of the universe. When He withholds things from us, He knows their absence is more important for our character. Since we cannot walk through life without the help of God, we may as well surrender and allow Him to walk us through it.

"I am the vine; you are the branches. If you remain in me and I in you, you will bear much fruit; apart from me, you can do nothing." John 15:5

SETTING ETERNAL GOALS

*"Since, then, you have been raised with Christ, set
your hearts on things above, where Christ is, seated at
the right hand of God. Set your minds on things
above, not on earthly things." Colossians 3:1-2 (NIV)*

The whole point of the Christian faith is to spend eternity
with Christ; nothing in the world can match that
expectation. With all we deal with here on earth, as
Christians and non-Christians, where we end up is
determined by our response to the cross of Christ. While we
can accept or reject Jesus, only our trust and obedience in
Him guarantees eternal Heaven.

My mother's love for Jesus was so tangible that even her
fight with occasional illnesses and dementia could not erase
Him from her memory. I recall the last time I saw her. As I
walked into her room, she was sitting on her bed, singing.
She looked at me and called me by my sister's name because
she could not remember who I was. I have known her to sing

every time and everywhere, but I was baffled by her ability to recall the words to different hymns when she could not remember her daughter's name.

When I became a Christian in my teens, it was natural for me to pursue the beauty of the relationship I knew my mother enjoyed with Jesus. Through her, I learned that God's love is eternal, with roots too deep to be pulled out by any sickness or persecution. Although Mum's life was far from perfect, her love for God was consistent, and she expressed it through unwavering devotion to the basic tenets of the Christian faith: prayer, worship, evangelism, and studying the Scriptures.

Today, Christianity is so watered down that it makes me long for the beauty of the simplicity of following Christ. Our focus shifts from all that truly matters, and we ramble around for clarity on things already answered in the Bible. We give preeminence to temporal things over eternal goals and simplify the cores of our faith while magnifying immediate gratifications. I am stretching for the height of trust I knew my mother had. A love so intimate that He was her greatest passion, even in her down moments.

As a Christian adult, I understood why the billows could not upturn my mother. She understood that her journey on earth was for a while and that her goal was to enter heaven victorious. All her troubles were too minimal to shift her focus from Jesus. Her death was painful, yet most comforting. That day, I knew exactly where she was and was grateful. She finally got to rest from her years of fighting sicknesses and the inconsistencies of life.

While we must enjoy our time here on earth, I do not want to get so engrossed in my desire to make earth comfortable that I lose focus of my final destination with Jesus (read "Heaven is home"). More than all legacies, I pray for the grace to pass the beauty of Christ's love to my children. I want them to know that, as Christians, we are in a race that leads to a specific place—heaven. Above all gratifications, I want them to rejoice in the hope of eternity with Jesus.

PART II

LEAVING FEAR TO LIVE IN THE FULLNESS OF PEACE

The Merriam-Webster dictionary defines fear as "An unpleasant, often strong emotion caused by anticipation or awareness of danger." No matter the form it takes, fear is unpleasant and sends our minds to the darkest alley of thoughts. Fear connives with our insecurities and limitations to render us hopeless. It leaves us mentally shaken and out of control. Fear envelopes and muddles the past with our present, making the future bleak.

I have known fear for as long as I have known my name, and before I had a savior to surrender my fear to, fear governed my mind like the Commander—in—Chief of my joy. It made me a prisoner to my past failures and a coward to my future exploits. It was the most dominating part of my emotions and raised its ugly head in the most unlikely situations. Before I saw the stars in the sky, I saw the darkness surrounding them, and the waves of the sea looked more terrifying than majestic.

Fear was a constant companion and an unwanted guest in every life decision. It raised the 'what ifs' and left me drained before I made any major life move. It was more than a disdain for spiders or heights. It was living in the bondage of an unknown instead of the beauty and fullness of the present.

Knowing Jesus changed my life, passion, emotions, and expectations. While it did not dispense my fears, salvation aligned it with God. So, in place of fear, I see God in everything, and my nights are no longer dominated by the 'what ifs.' I live conscious of the presence of a loving father. My challenges are no longer defined as failures because I know the God I serve. When fear demands my heart, I take it to Jesus and allow Him to walk me through the maze. I am on a journey that leads to Heaven, and any imbalances in my life are less intimidating.

Regardless of your genuine fears, you can lay them all at the cross of Christ and allow God to guide you through overcoming them. As you continue to lean on Him, your fears become His—reduced to nothing in the presence of God. Through faith, our fear is replaced with the assurance of 2 Timothy 1:10 (NIV), *"But it has now been revealed through the appearing of our Savior, Christ Jesus, who has destroyed death and has brought life and immortality to light through the gospel."*

Salvation connects us to Christ's victory over death, lifting us above the snare of fear.

WE WIN!

L ife is a battleground, a mysterious obstacle course filled with thorns, muddy paths, and "unthreadable" turns. The lights on the trails come on and off without warning, and different forces throw darts at you as you journey through. While each person's course might look different from others, we all have to navigate through its highs and lows. No matter who you are or your earthly worth, there is a piece of the action to go around.

Most people approach their unmapped paths defeated and deflated because they depend on their strength. They rely on human abilities, wisdom, wealth, and riches to carry them through the confusing maze. However, even after we master the art of "making it work," our feeble legs waver under the pretense because they cannot sustain the weight of it all.

Whenever my life turns unexpectedly, there is always that overwhelming sense of "not again." I wish the light of life would always stay on, with the birds singing and people praising. However, just when I think I have finally pulled through, heaved a sigh of relief, and got ready to take a long nap, the battle alarm rings again.

If it weren't for Christ, life would have screwed me in and left me for vultures to feed on.

If our stories are anything like the Avengers movies, the end would be predictable—the good guys win, and the bad guys get knocked down by Thor or smashed by Hulk. However, the perfect end to any man or woman's life has nothing to do with our self-virtues or moral accolades.

His devotion to His saints explains the unrelenting faith we have at the heart of the battle. Despite the weight and pain deep within, there is an unshakable assurance of God's presence with us, even when confined to a corner. Jesus said in John 16:33 (NIV), *"I have told you these things, so that in me you may have peace. In this world, you will have trouble. But take heart! I have overcome the world."* Knowing that we win, no matter how long the battle lasts, puts us ahead of the game.

We are not ignorant of what the world throws at us because Christ prepared us for the battle.

As His redeemed, we need this constant reminder that irrespective of our present or future battle state, God wants us to relax and enjoy the ride on His wings. Deuteronomy 31:6 states, *"Be strong and courageous. Do not be afraid or terrified because of them, for the Lord your God goes with you; he will never leave you nor forsake you."*

Guaranteed, through His death and resurrection, our victory was perfected in Christ. Although this life is momentary, God is with us through every step we take. The creator of Heaven and Earth stands on our side of the battle, and despite all the forces fighting against us, as heirs to the throne of grace, WE WIN!

The perfect ending can only be scripted by the blood of Jesus, a story dotted in red, and only in Him can anyone find true peace.

HOPE, WHEN YOU HAVE NOWHERE ELSE TO TURN

A while back, I received news that overwhelmed me to the point of exhaustion. It was like being in a cage with all doors locked and the keys far from reach. I paced from one room to the other, sitting for a while, then standing again. I was incessantly looking for a place or a position that would soothe my pain. My silly heart thought a beautiful view or some level of physical comfort would reduce my fear of the unknown.

No matter what I did, I could not run from my thoughts, which drained me. I wanted my mind to be blank and free from being bolstered by the negative possibilities birthed by the news. As the day dragged on, each way of escape my mind came up with sent me back to the corner of fear. As I sat on the floor, my hands over my head, I knew the only thing left to do was to ask for help from the only one capable of pulling me out of the mess: God.

I closed my eyes for a minute and simply asked Jesus to put the puzzles together and clear the fog so I could see Him clearer in the situation.

In that instant, Isaiah 41:13 (NIV) became real to me. God was lovingly telling me, *"For I am the Lord your God who takes hold of your right hand and says to you, Do not fear; I will help you."* He reminded me I was not alone and that He was holding me up, though it did not feel like it.

Regardless of the situation, I felt a calm that comes only from knowing you are in God's hands, and He will not let go. Of course, there was no wand waving, nor was there a puff of air that changed the reality of my predicament; however, nothing meant more at that point than the reality of God's role in my life affairs.

My situation did not change, but my view shifted to the Almighty God, who holds the entire world in His hands.

Proverbs 29:25 states, *"Fear of man will prove to be a snare, but whoever trusts in the Lord is kept safe."* I know what fear feels like; it starts with a thought and, if permitted, becomes a screaming mountain. However, through my walk with Christ, I am learning that fear does not have to linger. Instead of allowing it to grow into a menacing giant, I can shrink it through the washing of the Word of God and fortifying myself in prayer and worship.

That was not the last time I did the pacing and panicking, but with God's assurance that day, my understanding broadened. If nothing more, I have a permanent view of a loving Father carrying me above the waves. He is bigger than that medical, family, emotional, or financial situation and is committed to ensuring they do not destroy us. He's got this, and He's got your back. Hang on as He walks you (sometimes slowly) through the cracks and twists of your emotional roller coaster. In retrospect, you have so much more to gain by sticking with Jesus Christ than you will lose by enduring the pain.

COMFORT THROUGH WORSHIP

I still remember details about that day as if it were yesterday. I received a call from my uncle, asking me to stop by his house when I got off work. It was not the first time I visited him and his family. As I left for his house that evening, there was no way I could have guessed the intensity of what was about to hit my heart.

I could only expect he missed my pretty face and wanted to catch up. However, the news I received changed my view on life. After a quick chat, he told me that earlier in the day, he received a call that my brother just died. If there was ever a time I had an out-of-body experience, it was that day. Until that night, I thought death was for older people and those distant from you. I was in my late twenties, but it was my first loss, and the pain was indescribable.

I questioned my uncle, and none of the answers to the why, how, or what reduced my pain. I was so unprepared for the hard squeeze on my heart that I had no clue how to deal with it, and all the questions were jumping through my mind.

What will happen to Mum, and how would the news of the death of her first son affect her already frail mind? I could not blame God because I knew it was not His doing. Nonetheless, I questioned how God could allow me to feel the immense pain that gripped my heart, and the thought of waking up each morning was unbearable.

Often, we forget how much God is mindful of us, and in our quest to alleviate our uncertainties, we ignore the Father's soothing touch.

We blind our eyes of faith momentarily and surrender to the pressure of our present predicament. We nudge off that gentle tug that reminds us we are not alone but loved by a gracious God. Psalm 46:1b (NIV) states, *"God is our refuge and strength, an ever-present help in trouble."* As children of God, He is committed to ensuring we pull through all the challenges of walking through life.

Going to church the Sunday following my brother's passing was simply a circumstance of having "nowhere else to turn to." I did not expect a simple act of worship to be refreshing enough for my wounded heart. I did not want to dance, but I felt such relief in worship that I did not want to stop. My Father held me, but unrestricted were the tears that poured down my face. I realized that as I worshipped, my focus was more on Jesus. It made me more conscious of His presence and tenderness, reducing the pressure of my discomfort.

The pain was present, but so was God, and the joy of knowing that I had the Almighty holding me at such a time became an anchor for me. Sixteen years later, I still cry sometimes because I miss my brother, and God does not judge me for that. He is committed to standing by me for as long as it takes me to heal.

The act of worship is not tied only to the pleasant moments of our lives but to our determination to honor God regardless of the dictates of the moment. Like the fig tree without leaves and the vine without grapes (Habakkuk 3:17-18), I will rejoice in His presence regardless of my present situation. Through worship, we enjoy the majesty of God's splendor, leading us to experience a wealth of joy despite our pain.

I lost another brother just a few years later and then my mother. While each loss was as painful as the first, I knew where to turn to—God's presence. I have tasted the comfort and joy that come through worship from my first loss, and I now crave it as my sacred place. It weakens the catalyst for the pain and magnifies my focus on Jesus. Worship is more than how I feel: joy, gratitude, pain, or weakness. It is about trust in the God I cannot see yet honor with my emotions.

I find peace in the fact that, through worship, I can face many mornings because God's strength is perfected in my weakness as I worship.

YOU ARE ENOUGH!

If you have ever filled out one of those forms, informing people about yourself at the DMV (Department of Motor Vehicles), the passport office, or at the bank, your identity is summed up with about ten checkmarks. You are defined by the color of your skin, your age, your address, your salary range, your gender, and a few more things. I have checked those boxes many times and have default responses to each question without needing to read them.

In fairness, the questions significantly represent you—at face value. However, there is so much more to a person than others can see. There is a story before the story and many stories within the story. The journey did not start the day you were born; it started with you and God as the main characters of a bestseller. Before He formed you, God knew you. Your life is not a chance event but a masterpiece in the hands of your creator.

Before becoming the great prophet, it was difficult for Jeremiah to accept his mission. He did not even think he was suitable for the job when God called Him. Like all of us, he gave excuses for his limitations and concluded that being an ineloquent only child disqualifies him. God reminded him in Jeremiah 1:5a, *"Before I formed you in the womb, I knew you; before you were born, I set you apart."* He was chosen to be a prophet before he learned to say his name and all his inadequacies were irrelevant to God.

There are more parts to your story than anyone can see, and God looks beyond the ordinary to draft the extraordinary story of your life. Being black, white, a teacher, a woman, a man, a father, a mother, a sister, an American, or a Somalian are all parts of a larger puzzle. You do not need to be a certain race, a particular gender, part of a specific family, or have a particular job to fulfill God's plan for your life. You are all God needs because you are enough for Him.

Stop listening to the devil's lies because he has mastered the craft of deceit. He narrows the worth of people's lives to a single factor in a thousand lists. He leads them to believe they are worthless until that one thing is exactly what they imagined. He alters their mindset and shifts their focus from God, leading them to sum up their lives in a few factors.

God does not need our approval for the sufficiency of His grace, nor does He need to consult our checked boxes to use us. He will guide you through the bumpy rides and clear the foggy clouds as you allow Him to lead you. You are enough! Just as you are, and the devil is no match for God's plan for you if you trust Him to walk you through life.

No one but God has the right to define you because all they can see is a few pages in a thousand chapters.

HEAVEN IS HOME

With the voices all around me, it's easy to forget that my journey is beyond this world. I am conscious of embellishing my life's earned treasures in my walk with Jesus. My faith is at the core of all that I am, but the pulls and shrugs of sin and immorality in the world leave me panting and gasping for breath. Am I created to wiggle through these narrow thorns and accept the prickling pain of seeing people move farther away from God, or should the hurt lead me back to Calvary?

As Christians, we are compelled by the gravity of Christ's suffering on the cross and the joy that comes from knowing Him to devote our lives to the cause of Heaven— leading people to and not away from Christ. We can't explain away wrong with innuendos just to be applauded by the crowd. God loves people but hates sins (Isaiah 64:6), and regardless of how our emotions respond to it, God cannot be converted because He is perfect and Holy. He said of

Himself in Malachi 3:6, *"For I am the LORD, I change not."* He does not owe man any explanation, for He is sovereign.

We cannot wish away the tenets of our faith while declaring freedom because true freedom comes from walking with God. Our example is perfected in Christ, and our response should be brokenness for a world we know He died for. The Church should lead like Christ, extending grace but standing for righteousness.

Conformity to the dictates of men is not an option for survival because it ignores the echoes of Calvary just to be accepted. If Jesus Himself told us in John 16:33 that we should expect tribulations in the world because our peace is in Him, why do we seek affirmation and approval from people we should be leading to Him and pointing to eternity? We are not part of the crowd, but Heaven's advocate and our stance should mimic just that.

There is so much beyond life's last breath; how we live now determines where we spend it. I love this saying in my language, *"Aye loja, orun nile,"* which means, "The world is a marketplace, and Heaven is our home." No matter how long we live, there is an end date to our time here, and while God intends for us to maximize and cherish each waking moment, we must live conscious of eternity.

FIGHTING RIGHT: JESUS OR BARABBAS?

I've heard the story of Jesus and Barabbas, which has been narrated too many times to count. It is at the center of every salvation discussion and the core of many Easter messages. The story stimulates empathy for a man who knew no sin and was condemned to a gruesome death. It channels our hearts to focus on the crown of thorns on Christ's head and the blood dripping from every part of His body. It reminds us of the 39 lashes He endured before they paraded Him. It transports us to that day, standing with the crowd screaming "crucify Him," while He stands silent, determined to take it all.

However, Barabbas was not just a prisoner either. Matthew 27:16 (KJV) introduced him as "a notable prisoner." He was in prison for doing something that today would have earned him the support of many. To the Jews, he was more of a savior than Jesus was. He was a man ready to take on the Roman establishment in his bid to ease the suffering of his people. He fought for what was right—the minority—his clan. He was a hero! He was the Robin Hood of the Jews, zealous and fervent in his fight for freedom.

As I read Matthew's account of the event leading to Christ's crucifixion, I cannot help but notice the similarities in all that is happening today. We have so many Barabbas fighting for "noble causes," people who are clamoring for respect and the battle of the races to balance the equity equation, and we have all adopted the "live or die" approach to things we are passionate about.

Why was this story not different? Why is Barabbas a hero? Why not a callous murderer who truly deserved to die? Like every story in the scripture, it carried more weight than the literal. Jesus stood before the crowd, and they had only two choices. Choose an innocent man whose offer of love and salvation extends beyond the borders of Israel, or choose a man whose life's mission is to fight for an immediate gain: their right and their freedom.

Choosing Barabbas would have meant the death of a hero. It is a sad ending to a seemingly perfect movie plot—the death of a man who champions a worthy cause. Jesus was an easier choice to crucify because although He was one of them, lived with them, taught them, and served them, He was not like them and did not reason like them. He was different and did not say the things they wanted to hear. He promised a Kingdom they could not comprehend, made God too close for comfort, and expected them to love their enemies—He was a bigger threat than the Romans.

The moment you accept the gift of His salvation, you choose Christ over everything and become part of a global force. You are no longer limited by the things that define you here on earth. You are a Christian carrying the emblem of Christ's sufferings and the glory of His resurrection. You fight for what is right not because it is viral and has a million views but because it touches God's heart.

If our goal is to make Heaven, we must shake off the Barabbas in our minds, fighting for a few when we are called to fight for all. Our churches must reflect Revelations 7:9-10, extending our love beyond people who only look like us, *"After this I beheld, and, lo, a great multitude, which no man could number, of all nations, and kindreds, and people, and tongues, stood before the throne, and before the Lamb, clothed with white robes, and palms in their hands; And cried with a loud voice, saying, Salvation to our God which sitteth upon the throne, and unto the Lamb."*

Yes, we should live for justice and equality, but we must do so within the perimeters of our faith, fighting for what is right in the sight of God at all times, even if it means standing with people who do not look like us. We must display the God-kind of faith, which transcends skin pigmentation, geography, physical disabilities, social class, and worldly assets. We must have a faith that puts us right beside Jesus, choosing death for an undeserving world instead of the approval and applause of a group.

When He walked this earth, there was more to Christ than the statistics that defined Him. He was more than a Jew, a man, a carpenter, a teacher, a good person. He helped a fisherman (Matthew 4:22), healed a leper (Matthew 8:1-3), raised a friend from the dead (John 11:1-16), and responded to the need of a Roman soldier to heal his servant (Matthew 8:5-13). He dined with sinners (Mark 2:13-17), fed the crowd (Matthew 14:13-21), healed the sick (Matthew 8:16), and ministered to a stranger (John 4:5-29). He stood for all, spoke to all, and died for all.

All the people who shouted, "Crucify Him," might have believed they were leaving a worthy legacy for the coming generation. They did the right thing, choosing Barabbas over Jesus. They might have been proud, standing with "a hero." But we know they choose wrongly, condemning an innocent man to death.

Just because it is popular does not make it right. Jesus was not crowd-approved then and sure is not now. Pause before you raise the next placard or wiggle your fist. Are you standing where God wants you to stand? Think of Pontius Pilate standing between Jesus and Barabbas, asking, Jesus or Barabbas? Then make your choice—the hero Barabbas or the bloodied Christ.

Unless we understand our place as Christians and our role, we might end up fighting the wrong battles and joining in chants that break God's heart.

AS I WAIT

W e have all been there—the unbearable long wait to get a paper signed or prayer answered. Waiting for the sea of traffic caused by a pothole or an accident we did not cause. No matter the time or place we experience waiting, it is just not fun. It makes the clock tick slower and wears out our patience.

I have had to wait for many things, and I cannot say I have enjoyed them. A few of those are the nine-month pregnancy wait for each of my children and the long years it took to get a college degree. Like you, I struggle with waiting, and although I always get to the other side of the pain, each time I wait, it always feels like it will never end.

I am presently in one of those waiting periods and find myself telling God what to do and what I believe He is missing, neglecting that He is all-knowing and kind. I allow worry to replace supplication as my mind brushes off His command in Philippians 4:6: *"Do not be anxious about anything, but in every situation, by prayer and petition, with thanksgiving, present your requests to God."* God is ever faithful, yet I treat my situation like the first He has ever dealt with.

We are saved because Jesus waited. He started His journey as a baby and had to wait thirty-three years to fulfill His assignment. He chose a long road to Calvary just to die. Think about the agony of knowing why He was here, what He would go through to rescue us from our sins, and how long He will have to wait to get the job done.

Christ endured the wait because of the joy of seeing the cross become the symbol of salvation for the world (Hebrews 12:2). He understands when we pester Him about launching us to the next phase of life, and He does not flinch at our tantrums to get us out of a messy situation.

God is a good Father, and more than anything or anyone I know, He is mindful of His children. As you send your supplications in waiting, remember you are not alone. Rest assured that He will never leave you. The Psalmist said in 46:1b, *"God is our refuge and strength, an ever-present help in trouble."*

Even while waiting, we are guaranteed His presence, so wait, and you'll get to the other side in due time.

EVEN IF HEAVEN IS NOT REAL

I was fifteen years old when I received Christ, and I can clearly remember the circumstances that got me on my knees in my brother's room. Being raised by Christian parents meant I knew who Jesus was and His amazing heroic story. I knew about Heaven and hell and prayed every morning and night with my family. I was morally stable and even knew the words to most church hymns because of my mother's love for them. However, I did not think it was important for me to embrace Christianity beyond my moral accolades until that afternoon in my brother's room; the fear of missing Heaven led me to Christ.

While my Christian journey started with the fear of missing a chance to spend eternity in Heaven, over time, it grew into the joy of living my life to honor Christ and spend eternity with Him. Do not get me wrong, the thought of Heaven still sends tingles down my veins. Knowing the streets are paved with gold makes me less in awe of the finest diamond on earth. I love the prospect of living in a place where fear would no longer exist and where worship is constant—a place without the devil's antics and where all pain would cease. But getting to know Jesus has given me more than my fear of hell can—I am a child of God.

Speaking to the Pharisees in John 10:10 (NIV), Jesus said, *"I have come that they may have life, and have it to the full."* If Christ promises us a full life when we come to Him, it means any life without Christ is incomplete because a part of us was lost in Eden. Accepting Christ reunites us with God. It satisfies our longing for a relationship with our heavenly father and awakens a part of our humanity buried by sin.

No matter what leads you to Jesus, when you know Him, you get more out of the relationship than you hope for. My journey started with a cry for mercy to save me from hell, but He gave me a bounty of love. I have enjoyed peace in tumultuous situations because He promised it in John 14:27. I have a friend to talk to and a shoulder to cry on when it's too late and dark to speak to anyone. Christ's love for me is more real than a billion placard or hashtag can offer. He is more constant than time and space; His presence is my surety.

I would be a fool to give up love so complete in Christ to embrace the despair and uncertainty life outside Christ offers. Yes, Heaven is more real than our world, but if all I get out of following Christ is the joy, peace, and oneness with God, oblivion to people without Him, I lose nothing. He did not promise me a jolly ride through the earth, but He did say

He will always be with me (Matthew 28:20), and that is a beam of light in the darkest alley.

Understanding the depth of the transformation that occurs when we surrender our lives to Christ gives a more holistic view of our journey. It becomes about where we are heading and how we live before we get there. The journey to Heaven starts with the first step you take toward Jesus and leads through a narrow path to Heaven's gate.

THE LADY ON THE HILL: DISCIPLESHIP WALK

"That is, that you and I may be mutually encouraged by each other's faith." Romans 1:12

It was a bright, sunny, and beautiful morning in April, and everything seemed perfect except that I had to go for a Discipleship Walk later in the day. I have looked for every excuse in my book because I did not want to go. My walk with God is steady, and I am devoted to expressing my faith unapologetically. It took a nudge from the Holy Spirit for me to sign up to take a whole weekend off and head to a place I had never been or wanted to be.

As my husband dropped me off that evening, all I could think about was how long my weekend was about to be. I consoled myself, knowing I would be with Christians and there would be time for worship and prayer. Little did I know I was about to take a leap with God and learn new things I did not realize I needed to know about my walk with God.

As we walked toward the building to sign in and drop off my bag, I saw a friend who seemed more excited about the prospect of my pending trip than I was.

I embraced Solomon's advice in Proverbs 4:23 to guard my heart diligently. But I have added people who should not be on the list. Aside from church and my life group, I have always loved my time alone with God; sharing a weekend with "strangers" was simply uncomfortable. I think better in solitude, so that evening, when I heard I still had about thirty minutes to wait for the drive down, I left the room and went outside to sit on a little hill. I needed to take all the alone time before I wiggled through the crowd for seventy-plus hours.

Seeing a smiling face walk toward me on the hill that evening was the beginning of the greatest warmth I had felt from that many people in one weekend. I will later learn that when Cierra looked back and saw me sitting alone, she knew I was at the event against my will and walked to me to help crack the ice that God melted through my different encounters that weekend.

After worship, God's love is my favorite thing to talk or write about. However, this weekend highlighted something God needed to correct in my perspective. It has been God and me for so long that even my favorite human (my husband) can only take a few steps beyond the walls I have built up to fellowship with God. I love the little room I have created for the Trinity in my heart, and I have lived my

Christian life thinking God loves to fellowship with Martha a little more than with other Christians.

It took a reluctant journey from a hill at Northview Church, Carmel, to the cold, wet road of Discipleship Walk 150 and sitting at Martha's table surrounded by a beautiful group of God's beloved daughters to see why I needed the weekend. As I looked at the faces of all the women around me, I saw my Father's glory shine through them. Through their stories, struggles, and triumphs, I received strength, and while none of us is perfect, we are each a masterpiece in the hands of a loving God who is relentless in His pursuit of us. I remember asking my roommate, "Why would anyone want to be anything but Christian?"

In my few years as a Christian, I attended conferences, revivals, Church membership classes, and even an intensive three-week Bible school, but this experience was different. It was the most intentional Christian crowd I have ever seen, imperfect people in God's perfect hands. Love flowed, grace abounded, and the joy of Heaven flourished. For a moment, you could forget the chaos in the world and partake of the beauty of being surrounded by fellow believers.

My life was positively altered at the Discipleship Walk because I needed the experiences for the next phase of my walk with God. That weekend, I picked up a bucket full of gold nuggets, starting with Cierra's intentionality in approaching the lady on the hill. I grew in love because I saw others express love relentlessly, and I learned from how other women had already passed different tests.

As Christians, we do not have to live in a bubble because staying there will rob us of the wealth in the many Christians God sends our way. Life's race comes with fierce winds, but we are not alone. God wants to enlarge us by breaking down all the walls we have built around ourselves. And while I treasure my secret place with Christ more than anything else in life, I am learning to allow others into that space sometimes and step into theirs, too. I am letting go to allow God to make me uncomfortable to comfort others and be comforted by them.

THE JESUS FACTOR

"As it is written, there is none righteous, no, not one."
Romans 3:10

The Jesus factor is rooted in absolution because His mission to die for the sins of mankind was once and for all. No man before Christ and after Him can compare to anything He represents. He was a perfect human, and He is a perfect God. Abraham is regarded as the father of faith but can't be compared to Jesus.

Living in a broken world and at odds with our maker, the weight we carry as humans is heavy, and we are sinking under it. Our emotions are messy and out of control because they are created to surrender to God. Our paths have become cloudy and difficult to navigate because they should lead us to Him. And the farther we walk away from Christ, the heavier our humanity becomes. God knows we were not meant to carry the weight and offered Himself as a sacrifice to free us from the entanglements, but we question His intent.

Our human instincts will always go off the rail each time we try to do the math of life on our own. It can't add up without God. We are imperfect mortals in need of a perfect Savior, and the death of Christ on the cross gives us a pathway to walking in His perfection. I have learned to stop trying to move mountains with my human efforts when I know I cannot even change the course of a molehill. Our lives can only be meaningful when there is the presence of the Jesus factor, and we need to stop seeking good in people instead of leading them to the only good in life: God.

Righteousness is not something I can achieve; it is something I received through my salvation in Christ. If you are looking for any good virtue in me, look at Jesus in me. If you see hope, love, peace, and rest in my life, trace them back to the cross. Christ owns the credit for any positivity I exude, and I cannot even try to be a good human because I already know I cannot live righteously in my strength. The Jesus factor makes all the difference in how I treat others and respond to the world around me. Although my humanity occasionally raises the ugly heads of pride and prejudice, the surpassing grace of God sees perfection in me because of Christ.

PERMISSION FOR WEAKNESS

"But he said to me, "My grace is sufficient for you, for my power is made perfect in weakness." Therefore, I will boast all the more gladly about my weaknesses, so that Christ's power may rest on me."
2 Corinthians 12:9

There are days I could run a thousand miles mentally, but there are also those days I take a long break because I can't even move a limb. Today, the paths I could see clearly yesterday are cloudy, and all I can feel are walls boxing me into a corner. My strength from the dawn of the day becomes weakness from the night's somber clouds, and I just want to sit and rest on my Lord's shoulders.

Paul's encounter with Christ is one of the most convicting stories in the Bible. He saw Jesus after His ascension despite his devotion to persecuting the Church. He became a champion of grace and redemption for the church after his encounter with Jesus. However, even he experienced what it felt like to reach a limit and bow to the need to acknowledge weakness. In verse 6 of 2 Corinthians 12, he said, *"Even if I chose to boast, I would not be a fool because I would be speaking the truth. But I refrain, so no one will think more of me than is warranted by what I do or say."*

Sometimes, the road before us becomes a maze where our humanity wrestles with God's divinity. We take the bundle of life's burden from God's hands, believing we can carry the weight alone. In turn, we exert so much pressure on our little hearts instead of entrusting all our burdens to the only one who can bear them. God permits weakness because He does not withhold His grace, regardless of our shortcomings. Like a child in her mother's hand, we sometimes need to shut our eyes, sleep on the Father's shoulder, and allow Him to display His strength through our weakness.

Even when everything in our bubble seems to be going the right way, the brokenness of our world can overwhelm our view of Heaven. The daily calls to duty in our homes, work, and life can negatively affect us and leave us scraping from yesterday's grace. The need to align our earthly demands with the desire to see mankind come to the knowledge of Christ can become daunting. However, like Apostle Paul, we can declare, *"For Christ's sake, I delight in weaknesses, insults, hardships, persecutions, difficulties. For when I am weak, then I am strong."* 2 Corinthians 12:10.

As Christians, we do not have to feign perfection because our paths are paved with grace; we only need to dwell under the shadow of God's wings as we grow in Him. Although navigating between Heaven's and Earth's borders is intricate, God does not want us to stay on the shores. He wants us to live beyond the edge and walk others through Heaven's gate despite our limitations. He is not appalled by our weaknesses and will carry us before our feet fail.

GOD LOOKS GOOD ON YOU!

"My flesh and my heart may fail, but God is the strength of my heart and my portion forever."
Psalm 73:26

As I walked into the hospital that afternoon, I did not know what to expect. My heart was racing because I was overwhelmed by the sight of the sick in the hospital. I did not want to be there, but I had to be. I was in college, and a few days earlier, I received a message from one of my high school friends that Rashida, a mutual friend, got in an accident and was hospitalized near my college.

That was not my first or last time in a hospital, but it differed from the regular hospital. It was an orthopedic hospital, and everyone there had a missing body part. Walking to Rashida's bedside, I saw my friend smiling and thought I must be missing something. As I got closer, the smile became broader.

Looking at her, I could not speak; I just sat beside her bed, crying. She looked at me and said, "I am okay." Of course, I could not understand that because I could see that one of her legs had been amputated. But she understood something that I did not; she was not helpless or disabled as I thought; she was a child of God and was enjoying the warmth of her Father.

This story keeps revitalizing me because that encounter profoundly impacted my faith. Rashida was a Muslim and had given her life to Christ a few years before we graduated from High School. Although I was also a Christian, what I saw in her that day altered my view about the worth of being a child of God. She was in pain from the amputation, but no one could see it on her face. She looked more radiant than anyone else around her, and her faith was the glow in a dark season of her life.

I was privileged to have seen her embrace Jesus as her Savior around the same time I became a Christian. But the joy my friend exuded radiated in the room; even the nurses attending her were influenced by it. In the face of the "Whys," she was overwhelmed with joy. The nurses said her attitude was exceptional.

One of the many blessings of Christianity is knowing the worth Christ places on us because it helps us trade the cloak of self, shame, anger, and reproach for the garment of the joy of being saved. God looks good on you, regardless of where you appear with Him or the filth the world throws at you. He adds more to us than all the world's wealth, fame, and pleasures. His glory dissipates all our fears, and His majesty drowns every imperfection that comes with our humanity.

It has been decades since I saw Rashida, and I do not know how she is presently faring with life or even if she is still here with us, but she left an indelible mark on my heart that day — a mark that ingrained in me a value for my salvation, that is worth more than life itself. I have raised my hands to sing "The joy of the Lord is my strength" many times, but I saw it boldly expressed that day despite a missing limb. She lost nothing because she had Jesus.

SOMEONE'S GOTTA PAY!

*God made him who had no sin to be sin for us so that
in him we might become the righteousness of God.*
2 Corinthians 5:21

I called all my kids to ask who had left things out of place in their play area, and as usual, the three answers were the same: "Not me!" I have gotten so accustomed to this that I have learned a few detective tricks to catch the guilty kid each time. I have lived with them all their lives, so to a large extent, I can predict who committed an act based on their personalities.

Taking responsibility for our actions is not just part of our human nature. Instead, we would pull the world down before accepting the guilty plea. We are color-blind to guilt, and nothing is ever our fault. Even when the evidence is stacked high against us, we deny the obvious, convincing everyone around us that the color is white when it is red.

Others and never us, usually cause the deterioration of our relationships.

The "Whodunit" game ingrained in humanity is evident in our daily denial of the responsibilities that surround us. We are always looking for who to blame or shift our faults on. When the bell rang for who would take the fall for the sins of mankind, Jesus raised His hands, answered in our stead, and paid the ultimate price at Calvary. He assumed the nature of man to live like man, walk the path that we walk, and die in the most shameful way any man could. The death of Christ on the cross was a once-and-for-all deal, and regardless of who you are, where you have been, the road you have traveled, or what you look like, the cross speaks loud and clear because Jesus hung on it for your sake.

Although our sinful nature leads to destruction, God's love for man is infinite. He left the comfort of Heaven to pave a path for us to reach Him through Christ. And everyone who accepts the gift and sacrifice of Jesus's death on the cross gets to plead "Not guilty" because you cannot charge two people for the same crime. 1 John 2:2 states, *"He is the atoning sacrifice for our sins, and not only for ours but also for the sins of the entire world."*

JESUS LOVES ME; THIS I KNOW!

"But because of his great love for us, God, who is rich in mercy, made us alive with Christ even when we were dead in transgressions—it is by grace you have been saved." Ephesians 2:4-5

It was another one of those episodes my mum had to go through. She had been sick off and on for years. But something about that night triggered me to ask why. Knowing how much she loved God and how many people I have seen God heal through her intersession, I could not wrap my head around why she had to be sick.

I have written about my mum's faith a few times because I am building on the foundation she laid for me. Although she went through more challenges than most people, her love for God was unwavering. Her life was centered around her walk with Him, and she went out of her way to extend that love to others. Her life was a relatable sample of what it means to have a personal revelation of God.

No matter what the situation in the family is, Mum sings. I have not heard that voice in years, but the melodies of the hymns I sleep and wake up to are ingrained in my heart. As a young girl, I found strength in her joyful and upbeat personality because she was more heaven-tuned than earth-tuned, even when things looked shaky. She trusted her heavenly Father's goodness; although her condition might not look it, her countenance did. She saw beyond what others could see, giving her peace that could only be traced beyond the confines of a world that did not treat her kindly.

Suppose you have been in a situation that overwhelms you to the point that you question why; you are not alone. Like anyone else, I do not get a pass to an easy life because life is a short, bumpy road compared to eternity. There were challenges behind me and even some around me now. However, I will trade them all for the joy that rests deep beneath my soul. A joy that flows from the river of life I inherited as a child of God. And while there are a million things I do not know, the one thing I do know is "Jesus loves me; this I know!"

PART III

THE GREATEST PROMISE - I AM WITH YOU

"So do not fear, for I am with you; do not be dismayed, for I am your God. I will strengthen and help you; I will uphold you with my righteous right hand…. For I am the Lord your God who takes hold of your right hand and says to you, do not fear; I will help you." Isaiah 41:10,13

My mother ran her race with Christ; now I am running mine with Him. While I do not doubt she loved me, I know she could not be everywhere with me, even when she was here. Because of the limitations of humanity, her presence was constrained by time and space.

Despite the diverse technologies that can bring people closer to our dispensation, we are still withheld by those limitations. While they can enhance physical proximity, they lack the ability to reach and touch internal disconnections. In summary, no human can promise to "Always be with you" because it is physically and mentally impossible. And while my dying words to my children can be "I will be with you," it's impossible to honor that commitment.

My mother is no longer here, but she left me with the greatest gift any parent can give their children - the joy of God's presence. I love my children and will do anything within the law and my power to make life easy for them. However, my expression of love has limitations, and I am passing on to them the gift I received from my mum.

I can promise them money, attention, and their favorite dinner every day, but my promise to always be with them is more emotional than practical. Therefore, my greatest joy is seeing my children follow and serve God. As they walk with Him, I know His presence guarantees a light along their path.

The treasure of God's presence supersedes anything the world offers. His glory outshines the sun, and His love shields all hate. When we walk conscious of God's presence, every burden feels lighter and all opposition inconsequential. God does not promise, "I will always look from afar." He promises, "I AM with you!" He is "The I AM," and regardless of our challenges or the weight we bear, He never leaves nor forsakes us.

If you are a child of God, pause to soak this promise. The great "I AM" is with you! A promise sealed by your father, no matter where you go or what stands before or behind you.

HERE' S THE DEAL ABOUT GOD

"The fear of the Lord is the beginning of wisdom, and knowledge of the Holy One is understanding."
Psalm 9:10

Sitting in the hotel's courtyard, I looked at the sea before me and saw its vastness. The waves come in with a roar and recede with precision as if commanded. I tried to catch a glimpse of the end of it, but the more I looked, the farther it became. The ocean was majestic yet tamed by God's greatness. It was a perfect reflection of the earth's beauty and the glory of its creator.

Later that night, sitting around a burning fire on its shores with my friends worshiping, awe washed over me because above all the splendor I could see lies an unfathomable universe. A universe so vast we can never reach its end, even in our minds. Humanity is summed up in the greatness of God, and we owe our very existence to Him.

Without Jesus, no one would be worthy to stand before the Almighty.

Here is the deal about God; some say believing in an invisible being does not make sense, but even the things we can see do not make sense. The farthest visible galaxy is billions of light-years away, one of the trillions we have seen, and they can only be viewed through observational technologies. There are also billions of stars just in our world's galaxy. If we have not seen much of God's creation, how can we see the beginning of God? In a tumultuous, uncertain, and unrelentingly confusing world like ours, it takes looking deep into your soul to see God, where He alone can satisfy the emptiness.

The very existence of evil affirms the goodness of God. And until we bow to His sovereignty, we are at the mercy of a rough ride through life. As I look at the sky each day, I see the hand of God in it. As I walk on land, I feel the touch of God on it. As I breathe the air I cannot see, I smell the fragrance of Heaven. In honor of His greatness and matchless glory, I echo the ocean's roar and bow with its waves to declare Christ, King.

There are no words to describe the greatness of God, but I reflect with David to say,

1. *"The heavens declare the glory of God; the skies proclaim the work of his hands.*

2. *Day after day, they pour forth speech; night after night, they reveal knowledge.*

3. *They have no speech, and they use no words; no sound is heard from them.*

4. *Yet their voice goes out into all the earth. Their words are to the ends of the world.*

In the heavens, God has pitched a tent for the sun." Psalm 19:1-4

LITTLE MESSAGE IN A BOTTLE

"His pleasure is not in the strength of the horse, nor his delight in the legs of the warrior; the Lord delights in those who fear him, who put their hope in his unfailing love." Psalm 147:10-11

As I sat in church that day, I was overwhelmed by all that life threw at me. Like other times when I've felt burdened by a weight too heavy to lift, I knew I needed God to help ease my weary heart. The worship and message were great, but I needed something more - a voice from Heaven or a tap on the shoulder by a hand I couldn't see to calm my storm.

After church, just as I was heading out with my husband, a woman stopped us and said God laid a word in her heart to share with us. She cried as she relayed the comforting message to us, and my heart melted instantly. My mental tears were silent, and the knocks on Heaven's door were private, but the woman speaking to us was an extension of my Father, and her role was to remind us that we were not alone.

Maybe not as outright, but I have experienced a few encounters like this in my walk with God, as many other Christians have. God does not have to speak to us through His vessels, but He does out of His abundant kindness. Now, when I am at junctions, where my legs become too heavy to move, and all I can do is sit at the foot of the cross, I ask God for a little message in a bottle to ease my burden.

There are still other circumstances where I want to scream but cannot utter a word or want to cry but cannot find the tears. Situations that are too daunting for me to see beyond the veil or the light beyond the tunnel. Regardless of how confined the corner I am boxed into, I am growing to know how to look for the little message in a bottle God sends to revitalize and energize me to keep fighting.

That experience was enough to carry me through that season of life, and while I could still see the heavy load before me, I knew who was lifting it. Our circumstances did not change that day, but my heart did because God sent me a message through a stranger at church, and through her tears, I saw my Father's compassion for me. He was closer than I thought, and He felt every pull my heart endured. I rested in His warm embrace and was encouraged to continue the race.

As you walk through the shores of life, be mindful of those little messages in a bottle God places on your path to strengthen your faith. No matter how dark the sky above us or how high the waves of the sea we are riding on, there are moments when the ray of Heaven shines on us to remind us that God is closer than a brother. Consciously look for those encounters each day and store them in a jar in your heart; you will discover that God delights in seeing you flourish and always sends the sun to brighten your day and the rain to drown your fear.

GROWTH INDEPENDENCE

"I am the vine; you are the branches. If you remain in me and I in you, you will bear much fruit; apart from me, you can do nothing." John 15:5

The human definition of growth lines up with our sense of independence. A baby is deliberately weaned from its mother to teach the baby how to survive without the mother needing to feed it. The more a child grows, the less dependent they are on their parents. However, growth in our walk with God is the opposite of our understanding of growth. Unlike the growth of a human child, the growth of a "God child" is measured in dependence, not independence. The more we grow as children of God, the more we depend on Him.

Growing in our walk with God means we run to Him for things we otherwise would have managed independently. It means we lean on Him for our needs instead of attempting to figure things out ourselves. While the human child is expected to grow away from the parent, for instance, attending school and eventually moving out of the parent's home, the Godchild grows closer to God. As growing Christians, we do not move unless God follows; we do not step into any venture unless God steps in with us, and we do not even respond to anything in life until the Holy Spirit prompts us to respond.

As I grow in my walk with God, I am learning to acknowledge my need for Him for every little detail of my life. I am learning that my weaknesses become strengths when I lean on Christ and that with the daily turmoil within, my emotions are subject only to the power of the cross. I am beginning to understand that I am created dependent, not on any man or my mortal abilities but on God. And I can only walk through every road I walk with His strength.

God does not train His children to face life with their own ability. He does not teach us how to ride the bike by releasing His grip; He holds on to the handle and never lets us go. His promise is clear in Joshua 1:5. He told Joshua, *"As I was with Moses, so I will be with you; I will never leave you nor forsake you."* Learning to become less self-reliant and more God-reliant is a show of strength and should be a daily aspiration for every Christian.

The more we grow with God, the more we depend on Him. The Holy Spirit trains us to be more aware of our Father's presence so we can live conscious of His ability to carry every weight from our shoulders. Our childlikeness with God is not a weakness but a reflection of our trust in Him. It means we understand that God is always able and capable, and nothing is beyond or above Him.

RUN YOUR RACE, BUT NOT ALONE

"Therefore, encourage one another and build each other up." 1 Thessalonian 5:11a

God has always used friends to keep me focused on Him and help me navigate through the complex curves of life. For every season I've experienced, there are people God placed around me to serve as sources of strength and vigor to my faith. I know that in my walk with God, my world would be a lot more difficult without others running the same race with me.

I cannot share my salvation story without referencing how it started with discussing Heaven among my high school friends or getting through college without how God blessed me with Christian friends Jane, Sarah, and Lanre. Even when I thought my yearlong after-college community service would leave me stranded, God surrounded me with "The family," Tola, Korede, Kola, Dupe, and others. We were in a strange land, a Muslim state in Northern Nigeria, but we spent several nights praising and worshiping in the open fields, attracting other youths who were curious about God.

Although I spent my youth service in a place where Christianity was unpopular, my fear became my joy because while I was far from home, I found refuge in my God-hungry community. Together, we prayed, danced, ate, laughed, and left a positive mark on the sands of the land because of our shared love for Christ. That year remains my most spiritually rejuvenating time because I learned that no matter the path I take in life, God is present, and His people are also there. It gave birth to my dogged resolve to follow Jesus wherever He leads me.

Indeed, my faith is rooted in Christ, but I am not created to walk alone. For each season of life, it is essential to honor the people God surrounds us with so we do not miss out on the treasures in each of them. I am like a kid in a candy store when I am with my godly friends because of the soothing oil they pour into my heart each time we spend together. Their hunger for God fuels mine; their godly wisdom reduces the noise in my life to a whisper, and their presence makes Heaven a little closer. In a world as dark and overwhelming as ours, God lights our path with the torch in each of our hands, and when we shine them together, our path become brighter, and we see clearly.

Godly friends enrich our lives and remind us of the joy of walking with Christ. They are stimulants to our faith's vigor. Though it might not always be a bed of roses with friends, as Christians, there is great joy in sharing our path to Heaven, running side by side.

BLESSED ASSURANCE

"He that dwelleth in the secret place of the Most High shall abide under the shadow of the Almighty... He shall cover thee with his feathers, and under his wings shalt thou trust: his truth shall be thy shield and buckler. Psalm 91:1,4

God has been dealing with me recently, reminding me of His might and majesty. There is nothing more significant than the power of God, and He can do above all we can ask or think. I am a child of God, who made Heaven His throne and the earth His footstool. He can move hills, change hearts, level mountains, and calm storms.

Living in the United States, it is easy to be clouded by economic and social possibilities and hide behind the working systems of my geography. America can make it easy to forget that I got to where I am and will get to where God is leading me only by His strength. God fought for me in situations beyond my strength, bringing peace to my raging storms. Walking with Him trumps every worldly promise because I have witnessed Him do amazing things in impossible situations and turn emptiness into abundance.

I was reading an article by Pastor David Jeremiah, and he referenced a conversation between an African chief and an American missionary. The missionary asked why African churches witness more miracles than American churches. The chief replied, "In America, you have blessed insurance; in Africa, we have only blessed *assurance*!"

If we look at Africa through the eyes of the economy, politics, and leadership, nothing works the way it should. However, as Christians, when we look at Africa through the eyes of God and what He is doing in His church, we will see that the mighty hand of God has never failed us. The fire for God is burning brightly in the hearts of many, and His praise ascends to the Heavens even when the enemy pursues behind. The Church of Jesus in Africa is growing, and Christians are walking in the calling of God over their lives.

The Church of Christ in Africa catalyzes some of the world's most remarkable global exploits: science, engineering, mathematics, and social sciences. Despite the limitations and the lack of access to credit lines, of the top ten, five of the largest Pentecostal Church auditoriums in the world are in Africa. Many young Christians who grew up understanding their identity in God are walking with God across the globe. They are making a difference in their fields of study and raising a generation of children positioned to change the world for the glory of the Father. The Jesus factor is changing this generation's mindset to live beyond the faults of the past generations and walk with integrity and empathy for others.

To the wailing mothers of Africa, wipe your tears, for the Lord is strong on your behalf, and He will keep you safe and watch over your children and your children's children. He will heal the land and restore your wasted places. God is your blessed assurance, your resting place. He will make something out of your nothing and crown your princes with honor. Regardless of the noise from the noisome pestilence surrounding your nations, they will bow to the roar of the Lion of Judah. He is your refuge, your shelter from the storm, and He will save you.

Turning point (2023, February 18). *Big Promises: The Promise of Protection*. Daily Devotional. Retrieved February 18, 2023, from https://www.davidjeremiah.org/magazine/daily-devotional?date=2023-02-18&tid=email_edevo-wknd-021823.

I USED TO BE YOU

"He saved us, not because of our righteous deeds, but because of his mercy. He saved us through the washing of rebirth and renewal by the Holy Spirit." Titus 3:5

Although I was raised by Christian parents, I've not always been a Christian. I was born in sin, with the desire for sin, and I lived in sin. As I became aware of my conscience, sin only bothered me to the extent that it hurt others, and if the law says anything is correct, then I'm good. I built my castle and ignored the nudging of the Spirit of God within, urging me to step beyond the acceptable laws to honor my creator with my life.

I believed in God at that young age but thought He was too busy to be mindful of me. Although my heart relentlessly tried to figure things out by itself, I was overwhelmed—by the weight—I didn't even know I was carrying. The world God blessed me with was beautiful but had little meaning to my weary heart. I searched for answers to my many questions in places and from people who could not help me.

In place of communion with God, I delved into a world where I could daydream and create perfection through my own eyes.

I was a good person by the world's standards because I never got into trouble. I treated people right and respected the people in my life. However, my soul was a rebel against the things of God. It ignored Heaven and wandered off into the abyss. I allowed my heart to rule and placed my desires above the desires of God. I was content with navigating within the confines of the law, marking my checkpoints in self-righteousness to grade myself.

It takes God to know God, and it takes a Savior to be saved. If you have not met Jesus, I used to be you, a morally upright, dreamy-minded, lofty-eyed, goals-seeking, good human. However, I was empty until Jesus came and changed my life, transforming me into a new being. He walked me beyond the veil of the law to live above the defined good of the world. He exchanged my selfishness for love and peace and always gave my heart a song to sing. Jesus released my soul from the abyss of emptiness and set my eyes on Heaven above.

I am no longer lost or displaced; I am safe in God's hands. And now, I am not indebted to the law because I now live above it with Christ. I am at the mercy of a gracious Father whose love is eternal and whose mercy endures forever. My heart no longer gravitates toward sin despite my human nature because I have an advocate in Christ Jesus, who gives me the strength to live above my limitations.

JESUS ON THE LAP

Then Jesus told his disciples, "If anyone would come after me, let him deny himself and take up his cross and follow me. Matthew 16:24

I heard a story from one of my pastors. He said that while standing in the hallway greeting people as they left the church after service, he shook a man's hand who attended service for the first time. Striking a conversation with him, he asked him how he enjoyed the service, and his answer was, "It was great, but I do not like Jesus sitting on my lap."

Most individuals would love to wrap Jesus up in a box and only unravel the package when they need something from Him. They want the "Feel good" side of identifying as a Christian without the sacrifice that comes with discipleship. They prefer the cradle of His birth to the cross of His death. They would rather sing "Bless me, Lord" than "I surrender all" and live to self than die to sin.

Following Christ does not entail laying on a bed of roses and sipping lemonade. Following Christ comes with a deep resolve to carry your cross and go where He leads. Before He told the disciples to follow Him in Matthew 16, He explained to them what would happen to Him in Jerusalem—how He would suffer and die on the cross. It was not a conversation that stemmed from "You will always be happy when you follow me." Jesus did not try to attract them by what He could give them physically but by the sacrifice He was willing to make to save their souls.

Jesus was telling the disciples that they had a choice: to follow or retreat. He was going to the cross regardless. Thinking Jesus was sentimental about His assignment to die for humanity, Peter assumed Christ's decision was up for debate. He called Jesus aside in Matthew 16:22 and told Him, *"This shall never happen to you!"* At that moment, Jesus knew who was speaking through him and said, *"Get behind me, Satan!"*

Most believers act like Peter in our walk with Christ. When everything is rosy and nice—we are healed, the children are doing well, and our mortgage is paid on time, we stick by Him, but when He calls for a sacrifice, we retreat and try to negotiate our way out. Although following Christ comes with all the beauty life could ever offer—love, peace, joy, freedom, hope, and grace, it also comes with a cross, and we must be willing to follow Christ with our cross. Jesus told the disciples in verse 24, *"Take your cross and follow me."*

The man who said he did not want Jesus sitting on his lap loved the singing and clapping in church. He enjoyed looking at the smiling faces but got uncomfortable with the call to surrender and follow Christ. I do not know if he ever returned to the church or found another church where Jesus was far, yet His goodness was near enough for comfort. Until we are willing to take up our cross to follow Christ, we cannot fully understand the fellowship of His suffering.

WHAT ARE YOU WEARING?

"Therefore, put on the full armor of God, so that when the day of evil comes, you may be able to stand your ground, and after you have done everything, to stand. Stand firm then, with the belt of truth buckled around your waist, the breastplate of righteousness in place, and your feet fitted with the readiness that comes from the gospel of peace. In addition to all this, take up the shield of faith, with which you can extinguish all the flaming arrows of the evil one. Take the helmet of salvation and the sword of the Spirit, which is the word of God." Ephesians 6:13-17

We spend so much time thinking about what to wear for different occasions, and putting our looks together takes effort. It also depends on where we are heading. It is easier to pick an outfit for movie time at home than for movie time out of the house. What we wear and how we wear it speaks volumes about our personality and destination. You do not wear a suit and tie when you go to the gym, and a soldier does not enter the battle arena wearing an ugly Christmas sweater with neon lights. This also applies to our spiritual garments; we must consider how we appear in life's arena.

I am not particularly a fashionista, but I love quality things because they last and retain their value longer. I will spend a little more on a round-neck tee shirt if I can get better value from it than spend the same amount on a complete outfit with less value. I apply the same principle to my walk with Christ. I weigh the value of all my benefits as a believer with the worth of losing those privileges for momentary gains.

As Christians, we need to decide who designs what we wear spiritually. Is it Christ or culture? Have we attached some add-on pieces to our faith as we journey, picking on embellishments that do not match Heaven's design? Just like no worldly designer will appreciate alterations to his/her design, God wants us to model His designs just as He made them as we walk through life's runway. He wants us to walk in truth, love, peace, righteousness, and integrity, holding on to our shield of faith so it can help us extinguish the flaming arrows all around us.

As children of God, we must look "the part" because how we show up in the world reflects where we are headed. Most individuals spiritually walk around in tattered clothes, forgetting the saying, "The way you are dressed is the way you will be addressed." We've become so accustomed to our world that we neglect that Heaven is our goal and our destination is flawless.

Many of us have set aside our armor, replacing the belt of truth with lies and our breastplate of righteousness with filthy temporal gratifications. Before we head out the door daily, we need to look through the mirror of Heaven and ask ourselves, "What am I wearing?" As Christians, are we living conscious of ungodly attachments to our spiritual garments, and are we intentional about allowing God to peel off our excesses and rip off worldly patches we have picked up along the way? What we wear as citizens of Heaven is vital, and it is on us to guard how we show up on the world's stage.

IF YOU ARE A CHILD OF GOD

"Can a mother forget the baby at her breast and have no compassion on the child she has borne? Though she may forget, I will not forget you! See, I have engraved you on the palms of my hands; your walls are ever before me." Isaiah 49:15-16

Discovering your identity is the bedrock of who you become. Growing up, my parents always told us to remember the daughter/son of whom we are. Although not physically present with us all the time, they wanted us to carry the silent creed of the family everywhere we went and to behave in manners that affirmed our upbringing. The values my parents instilled in me greatly influence how I approach the world around me.

While we do not always do everything to honor people who have poured godliness into us, the consciousness of where we come from and who we are determines how we relate to the world around us. It affects what we believe to be true and what is not. It fuels "The value of you," forming your identity and serving as the root from which your life sprouts.

A mother can forget her newborn child, but God can never forget you. Understanding who you are in Christ releases you from the bondage of seeking your identity in places they do not exist. It gives your spirit strong, beautiful wings to soar and it provides your weary soul a resting place. Knowing God is your Father calms your storms and fans your sails on the ocean of life.

If you are a child of God, you do not have to live in the illusion of who others believe you are or what they believe you are worth. You are a son/daughter of the Almighty, the Yahweh, the Ruler of the past, present, and eternity. Your name is written in the palm of God's hands, and He is always mindful of you, your struggles, triumphs, disappointments, and victories. His love for you spans beyond any man's imagination and runs deeper than the deepest end of the sea.

THE KINGDOM- MINDED CHURCH

"Then he said to his disciples, "The harvest is plentiful, but the laborers are few; therefore, pray earnestly to the Lord of the harvest to send out laborers into his harvest." Matthew 9:37-38

When I became a Christian, my first desire was to start attending church consistently. Although I attended church with my family on some Sundays because my parents were Christians, I could not attend as much as I would love to after I accepted Christ. We could only attend service a few times a month because we relocated farther away from the church, and we had to depend on the church's bus to pick us up for services. Being too attached to our church, Mum would not change to a closer church because she delivered her children and served for years in the church. However, weighing the benefit of my spiritual growth, she gave her blessing for me to attend a church I could safely walk to and attend services.

I chose the closest church because it was just a five-minute walk away from home. I loved being there and would go almost daily, even without a service. There is something about church that draws me closer to my Savior, and if I could live there, I would. A few months after my first service, I became a Sunday school teacher, youth choir leader, and the adult choir's secretary. As part of the youth teaching team, I taught my first message when I was seventeen. I remember my message was on Daniel's vision. At that young age, I wanted to serve Jesus in every capacity possible, and I dug into the Bible as if my life depended on it.

In my desire to continue to grow as a Christian while fully devoted to my roles at my local church, I started attending monthly seminars at another church because of my global view of Christianity. Being surrounded by other Christians hungry for God's word always felt encouraging. However, while I stood at my church's gate with the youth group one evening, the church's overseer drove in. When he called me, I thought he just wanted to say 'hi'. Instead, he said he heard I had been visiting another church, so he didn't want me to enter his church again. He mistook my allegiance to the church of Christ for loyalty to him and felt betrayed that I attended seminars in another church.

Imagine the blow to my young, hungry heart. I could not believe my seventy-something-year-old pastor had just sent an eighteen-year-old girl packing from church because she attends Bible seminars in a different church. That encounter broke my heart because it took me away from people I have come to love so dearly. It took my personal walk with Christ for me to keep moving toward my goal of making it into the presence of God despite my disappointment. I immediately joined another church and started the church immersion process again.

That was over thirty years ago, but I cannot help but wonder if bureaucracies in the church of Christ today are debarring people from serving their Savior in the capacity of His grace over their lives. I have had to cross many hurdles to continue the mission God started in my life years ago. I am now at a point where God had to give me a ministry that extends beyond the confines of a local church. After a few church membership classes, I am now tired of going through them each time we move.

These classes are perfect for new believers, but individuals who are already Christians need different immersion training. You do not keep retraining a soldier to swim in a lake when he or she is ready to deep-dive in an ocean. Secular organizations are doing a better job building off people's resumes and verifying their past to maximize their present.

There is one Christ, one cross, and one Heaven. All our efforts as a church should be coordinated to establish God's will on earth. As Christians, our salvation is final; it doesn't renew each time we change churches or relocate geographically. We're blood-washed, spirit-filled, and Heaven-bound, and we should join the local church ready to man our posts and grow the Kingdom.

While I believe in structure and order, I also believe that every believer is called to serve in the church in some capacity, and the number caps and defined service areas put in place by many churches are limiting. You can be a teacher, scientist, accountant, lawyer, or engineer for the kingdom. Each of God's callings is unique to each individual but with the same end goal of expanding His Kingdom and building up His people on earth for His glory. For instance, you cannot get the best from me as an usher because I do not have the grace for it, but my husband is perfect for that role. While some are great at welcoming people to church, I serve better in the background.

When an active Christian moves to our local Church, we need a "Continue button," not a "Reset button." The weeks spent in believer's class for a Christian will improve the church's well-being as a mission training class. While we cannot make room for all gifts, we shouldn't bury them. We can establish a process to help nurture and grow all God-given, kingdom-growing talents, even if they are used outside our local church. We should be ready to encourage and support, and if we need to build ramps to help crippled members sing in the worship team, we should build the ramps. Even if everything does not always fall within our structure, we can get all hands on deck, for Heaven's sake.

There are only two types of people in Christ-centered churches: saved and unsaved. Our mission should be to lead the unsaved to Christ and the saved to live for Christ. All the saved believers sitting on the rows of chairs are soldiers and should not just be fed to live the "American dream" behind white picket fences. There are souls to save, lives to touch, hearts to heal, and homes to restore. Plowing our Father's garden is not restricted to a selected few; it's a privilege we all get to share. I look around during each church service, praying that every unsaved person finds Christ and every believer takes up their armor to fight the good fight of faith. The bottom line is that the Church is more vibrant and alive when every Christian operates in the fullness of God's calling over their lives.

The Kingdom demands more than our limited church walls and structures can offer. We are the church of Christ; we represent one Kingdom and work together for the same purpose of lifting Jesus. We are not in competition or at odds because we have one Father, and we all have a common destination. There is a sense of urgency for Christians to unite and fight as one—an urgency that calls us all to live mission-minded lives.

We play hide, seek, and retreat games when we are supposed to occupy until He comes. In Act 1:8, Jesus said to the disciples: *"You shall be witnesses unto Me both in Jerusalem, and in all Judea and in Samaria, and unto the uttermost part of the earth."* The great commission starts from Jerusalem, in this case, America, before we can reach the utmost parts of the world with the gospel. The world needs Jesus, and the church needs all hands on deck to get the job done not just by sending aid to third-world nations but also by raising giants here in the West who are ready to raise the banner of Heaven until Jesus comes. Our faith should reach beyond the walls of our churches to impact the lost world.

Imagine if every believer who walks through the doors of every church is put to work in the capacity of God's grace for their lives and their journey and training maximized! Think of the spiral effect of all Christians living a kingdom-minded life and the transformations possible when we each impact an individual, who also goes on to impact another. There is a place on the battlefield for all Christians, but we are leaving many soldiers unassigned, forgetting it is all about Heaven. When the Kingdom wins, we win.

ALWAYS A WIN WITH GOD

"Show me your ways, Lord, teach me your paths. Guide me in your truth and teach me, for you are God my Savior, and my hope is in you all day long." Psalm 25:4-5

Severally, I have asked other people to meet me in the middle. It is just a civil way of finding common ground by reaching a compromise to gain something. When negotiating, people often ask to meet in the middle because no one wants to be on the losing end of a deal. Although a win-win situation is not always ideal or the best business deal, people prefer that because while you can lose some, you do not want someone else to win at your expense.

The rich man in Matthew 10 thought he could negotiate eternity with Jesus. He approached Christ as he approached his worldly deals. He wanted some form of compromise: give some and lose some. However, the Bible said, *"Jesus felt genuine love for him."* Matthew 10:21a. Jesus loved him already, yet he missed the purpose of his visit because he was not willing to surrender all to follow Christ. If Jesus had asked for some of his wealth to be given away, he would have left feeling great because he could still retain some while losing some.

There are no compromises to following God. You either follow Him wholeheartedly or you do not. You do not get to hold on to the things that separate you from walking in righteousness and expect God to meet you in the middle. Although He is willing to walk you through the process no matter how long it takes, you must be willing to let it all go.

The Bible says the rich man's face fell, and he went away sad. With all his possessions, he left dejected because he refused Christ's offer of eternity. Christ did not stop loving the rich man, but the rich man chose not to surrender to Christ. That was his choice.

Thriving human relationships are built on compromise, but God-man relationships are built on absolute surrender. It starts when we accept that we cannot do anything without God and lay everything down in surrender. God does not meet anyone in the middle; He comes to where we are, delivers us from our sinful nature, and only asks for our willingness to follow Him. He does not demand that we get clean. He waits for us to accept His will and He does the dirty work for us. He is gracious and merciful, and His love endures forever.

IF NOT GOD, THEN WHO?

*"For I am the Lord your God who takes hold of your
right hand and says to you, do not fear; I will help
you." Isaiah 41:13*

I was having a conversation with my daughter, and we
were trying to think of alternatives to serving Jesus. We
asked the question, "If not God, then who?" If the world
wants to pry me away from my savior, what alternatives does
it offer me? Regardless of how you weigh it, it simply makes
better sense to follow God.

There are alternatives to all the things we use daily. For
instance, I can use a tissue instead of a paper towel or swap
one drink for another. I can go to college, learn a trade, drive,
or ride a bus. We have choices for everything we need each
day, and there is just no one-size-fits-all for anything in life.

However, we have a single choice when it comes to
following God. You either follow God or you do not. This
choice has its roots in the fact that we were created by Him,

and in Him alone, we are complete. Although the world has relentlessly tried to offer alternatives to the satisfaction of walking with God, we are rattled by those choices because, without God at the center, the sphere of our lives gets distorted.

You do not have to mask it or clean your mess up before Christ accepts you to the fold of faith. He loves you enough to clean up all your mess, and you can come to Him just as you are. Any alternative the world offers will demand your effort and entail getting your acts together in your own strength. However, your salvation in Christ offers His grace and promises forgiveness, peace, joy, mercy, hope, faith, righteousness, love, unity, and eternity in Heaven. The world can never match this boundless grace God extends to us because it offers unrest, condemnation, hopelessness, sin, division, damnation, fear, and anxiety.

If not God, then who? What can anyone offer me that supersedes the grace, joy, and fellowship I enjoy walking with God? At nights when I do not know what to do and sleep eludes me, can anyone show up in the middle of the night and sit by me and ease my burden? If I give up the comfort and hope I have in eternity, do I have an alternative guarantee that outweighs the joy of Heaven? There is no alternative to God; choosing to follow Christ gives our lives meaning.

THE GIFT OF CHRISTMAS

"But the angel said to them, "Do not be afraid. I bring you good news that will cause great joy for all the people. Today in the town of David, a Savior has been born to you; he is the Messiah, the Lord." Luke 2:10-11

The events that led to the birth of Christ go against our mortal belief system. Despite our resistance to honoring Him, God was committed to His decision to offer Christ for the salvation of the world. Although Jesus could have received the most royal welcome, accompanied by a host of angels, to show us how far He would go for mankind, God allowed the events preventing His birth to occur without any interference from Heaven. While the devil tried to stop Him from stepping into the battle arena, Christ's entrance to the scene between mankind and the accuser ended our hopelessness.

What a joy the shepherds must have had when the angels told them about the birth of Christ. On an unassuming day, under the clear skies, they received the good news of the Messiah's birth. At that moment, in the dead of night, watching their flocks, they participated in the glorious entrance to earth of the Savior of the world.

Stepping down from glory to dwell among men, our king chose the humblest means to be born. Christ could have been born into the most influential household, but He chose a carpenter and a virgin girl. His birth could have been the headline story of the day, but it was in the backdrop of the brutal murder of the sons of wailing mothers. The echo of His birth could have been heard from across the world, but it was reserved for the lowly shepherds. Jesus could have been born with the sun shining on His face, but He chose to arrive in a manger at night.

The gift of Christmas keeps giving. No matter what is happening around us or the backdrop of our world, the spirit of Christmas spreads joy across the globe. It is not tied to worldly wealth, jingle bells, the beautiful flurries of snow, or the highest towering Christmas tree. "Christmas" is a gift from God that reminds us of the depth of God's love. After several generations, we are privileged to partake in the joy the shepherds must have felt in the wee hours of the first Christmas morning.

THE DEEPER YOU GET WITH GOD

"Now devote your heart and soul to seeking the Lord your God. Begin to build the sanctuary of the Lord God, so that you may bring the ark of the covenant of the Lord and the sacred articles belonging to God into the temple that will be built for the Name of the Lord." 1 Chronicle 22:19

Digging for treasures has been our world's staple, generation after generation. From beneath the earth and ocean, we have discovered some of the greatest elements that make our world function better. We have drinking water, oil, gold, cobalt, pearls, and many other resources because we venture to dig deeper than what the surface offers. Our crops bear fruits and leaves because their roots reach deep beneath the earth.

There is something about going deeper and seeking to know God more. Stepping beyond the doors that confine us behind our religious fortress ushers us into a life of adventure that comes from walking with God. The deeper you walk with God, the more of Him you find, and the more of God you find, the more of Him you desire. When you start digging deeper, it becomes impossible to stop because of the rush of discovering the mysteries beyond the veil.

In every layer, we peel off our selfishness and pride to unveil His godliness in us, and He rewards us with more peace and satisfaction than the world can ever give. Treasures beneath our humanity can only be revealed when we allow Christ to strip us of every filth and clothe us with His righteousness.

I started my journey with God over three decades ago, and the deeper I get, the more treasure I discover of His majesty. Unlike earthly treasures, which we mostly only discover when we get to the bottom, the treasures from seeking God start at the moment of salvation and continue with each scope of dirt we shovel off our lives. As we grow in our faith, we see Him more, and as we gaze upon His countenance, our lives are enriched with the light of His glory.

David found God early in life, but His desire to know God earned him the qualification of "A man after God's heart." Although he understood the omniscient ability of God, David also embraced His sovereignty over every little detail of his life. To him, God was more than a statue erected for momentary worship. He writes in Psalm 63:1, *"O God, you are my God, earnestly I seek you; my soul thirsts for you, my body longs for you."* Despite his mortal imperfections,

David allowed God to remove layers of dirt he didn't know existed in him. He started with God and ended with God because he continued to dig and seek God until his last breath.

PART IV

IF YOU CAN SEE WHAT I SEE

"The one who looks at me is seeing the one who sent me. I have come into the world as a light so that no one who believes in me should stay in darkness." John 12:45-46

The morality of humanity dwindles with each click of time. As Christians saddled with the responsibility to lead people to Christ, we struggle with balancing the act of expressing our faith and letting people see through our lens. I am as bold about my faith as any Christian, and there is always that nudge within me that wants to shake people up to see what I see. However, God has been dealing with me in the past few years to look at the life of Christ as my reference for approaching people who might be living in the dark or those whose lights are dimmer than mine.

The backdrop of the world Jesus lived in was as overwhelming as the one we live in today. He came through individuals who were oppressed and bullied by the Roman empire, and His father was a simple carpenter. Although He is majesty personified, He did not live a glamorous life on earth. Despite that, throughout His ministry on earth, Christ's message was not convoluted with the weight of the issues around Him because He knows that saving our souls is worth so much more regardless of what the world throws at us.

The familiarity of Jesus's conversation with the woman at the well expresses His nature to reach us where we are and to offer us the light that comes from walking with Him. He stepped out of the norm to reach a woman ignored and condemned by the people around her. Although He disapproved of how she lived, He did not condemn her either. Instead, He offered her a way out, showing her a lighted path to turn her life around.

The world is like a dark room with everyone walking around bumping into things, and when you become a Christian, you receive the light that opens your eyes to see the right order of things. However, sometimes, we forget that not everyone sees what we see, and instead of leading people to the light, we assume others should see what we see without pointing them to Christ, the source of light. If we point the world to Jesus and they accept Him, then people can see what we see as Christians, and they will understand that the love of God eliminates our need to lean on our own power to navigate a world as complex as ours.

THROUGH THE WINDOW OF GRACE

For the grace of God has appeared that offers salvation to all people. It teaches us to say "No" to ungodliness and worldly passions and to live self-controlled, upright, and godly lives in this present age." Titus 2:11-12

I found myself caught up in the web, spurned by all the distractions and noise in the world. Like many Christians, I built a cocoon and nestled in it instead of standing on the steps of grace to invite others to follow the path that has given my life meaning and hope. Over time, it has become easier to have a haughty attitude toward my salvation, forgetting I was saved by grace and grace alone.

While I agree that our present world needs Jesus, the fact remains that the world has always been at odds with God's definition of living righteous, yet Christ chose to die for mankind. Through His journey, Jesus encountered an adulterer (John 8:1-15), a demon-possessed (Mark 5:1-20), and His feet were soaked with tears and wiped by the hair of a prostitute (Luke 7:36-39). Christ was surrounded by broken people, yet He extended grace to all. He accepted everyone willing to embrace His forgiveness at every chance, even while hanging on the cross.

We are saved by grace, and looking at the world through the window of grace pulls us out of our comfort zones as believers. It leads us to individuals who were condemned by our proud hearts as our Savior calls for salvation. It makes Heaven closer, compelling us to leave the door to the grace we enjoy open to others. It also brings individuals who seem distant from God closer to forgiveness.

God's grace is constant and sufficient for all our shortcomings. He is not overwhelmed by anything, and there is nothing man can do to displace the abundant love of Christ—not the uproar, the uncertainty that plagues our world, the wickedness of man against man, or the immorality that besieges our mortal hearts. The love of God stretches beyond our limitations and extends beyond the galaxies. He never despaired from chasing after us because He knew what we were before He chose to step into hell to save our souls.

A MILLION AND ONE REASONS

"Praise the Lord, my soul; all my inmost being, praise his holy name. Praise the Lord, my soul, and forget not all his benefits—who forgives all your sins and heals all your diseases, who redeems your life from the pit and crowns you with love and compassion, who satisfies your desires with good things so that your youth is renewed like the eagle's." Psalm 103:1-5

Although we might be surrounded by waves threatening to drown us, there are a million and one reasons to be grateful to God. His love speaks through the sun that shines every morning and the moon that lights our sky at night. His grace breaks through our imperfections, and His mercy cuts through our limitations.

When we think of all the events happening in the world, we might lose sight of the need to acknowledge the creator who is still holding it all together. Even in the presence of guilt, His mercy cuts through. God is the only constant;

generation after generation, life and godliness have prevailed over evil. He has the world in His hands; regardless of how far we are stretched, He will not let go.

The God of the universe is mindful of humanity; regardless of our circumstances, God is good. It is by His grace that we are sustained. He is ever faithful and dependable, and His love endures forever. When we think of His goodness, we are reminded of the nights He wipes our tears away, the ditches He rescues us from, the mountains He levels before us, the rivers He parts for us to cross, the roads He paves for us to walk through; the heights He helps us attain, and the many battles He keeps winning for us. So, despite all oppositions, we are grateful to the Most High God for innumerable reasons.

PERFECTION FROM A SHARPENED LIFE

"But he knows the way that I take; when he has tested me, I will come forth as gold." Job 23:10

I'm not an artist by any means, but my daughter is. She loves art and picked up drawing at an early age. For every birthday, she makes the most beautiful and personalized art. It is just a form of relaxation for her and serves as a means to express herself.

To encourage her interest, I always buy her drawing pens and pencils. She loves seeing well-chiseled pencils because they make the drawing experience easy and clear. She has an electric sharpener on her desk, and you will know she is creating something new when you hear the gritting sound of the pencil going through the sharpener. For every page of art she draws, her pencils go through the process multiple times.

Job's story is one of extreme circumstances, but we can all relate to his despair and confusion. He lost it all but still had it all. Although he was unaware that God allowed the devil to test him, he focused (mostly) on his maker.

It is not pleasurable to endure trying times and contend with forces you cannot see. However, each time you make it through a round of opposition, your faith grows taller, and your trust becomes a little wider. In such times, God is making a perfect art out of your life. Like a pencil in the hands of the master artist, you might have to go through the sharpening process multiple times before the picture of your life becomes the star of the gallery.

Most of us are living on the steam from our past encounters with God. We are drafting our stories with dull ends instead of allowing God to sharpen us, removing the excesses barring Him from accessing the perfections within us. In place of total surrender to His will for our life, we assume the role of critic before the end of the story. Just because everything looks blurry when we go through trying times does not mean God is done with us; we are simply going through a sharpening process. And although it hurts, it prepares us for the next angles and curves God wants to walk us through as He draws the perfect lines of the big picture.

CHURCH LIKE HEAVEN

"Just as a body, though one, has many parts, but all its many parts form one body, so it is with Christ. For we were all baptized by one Spirit so as to form one body—whether Jews or Gentiles, slave or free—and we were all given the one Spirit to drink."1 Corinthians 12:12-13

When my family moved to the United States, we attended a church that felt like our church in Nigeria. We wanted to enjoy the same praise and worship style, mingle with people who spoke our local language, and pray as we did. While we loved the church, after a few months, I got restless because I wanted more than the cultural feel of a church.

I realized that no one I met in my after-Sunday activities looked like the people I sat with at church. It limited my overall viewpoint on what Jesus said in Matthew 15:15, *"Go Ye into all the world..."* The understanding that I was first a citizen of Heaven before I was Nigerian made it uncomfortable for me to surround myself with only Nigerian Christians in a diverse society.

With that realization came a desire for my global Christian identity to reflect in my decisions about every aspect of my life, including church selection. I wanted to see God in the people I met at the grocery store, on the streets, and in my daily life. I did not want to be blinded by my cultural view of Christianity and miss out on great relationships with the children of God.

In addition to aligning my identity with our local church selection, my husband and I knew we would be raising our children in the United States, and we did not want them to grow up believing Christianity was limited to their parents' culture. After all, Christ died for the world, not just Nigerians. We live here, and we wanted them to experience church, like Heaven, where culture, skin color, and wealth status are no barriers.

The family of God extends beyond the confines of our predetermined worship styles and church traditions. Our compass for navigation should be structured between the lines of the scripture and not our church's cultural artifacts and history. Christ died so that "all" might be saved, and regardless of how different the believer sitting next to you in the church is, you are bonded by a cord stronger than geography or demography. You are family by virtue of your salvation through the sacrifice Jesus made at Calvary.

While the role of Indigenous churches in Christendom cannot be overemphasized, it is vital that we remember that the goal of any church, regardless of its location, is to preach Christ. Our values are rooted in Jesus and Heaven, not boundaries drawn by man. Yes, it's acceptable to mind the details of our local churches, but in doing so, we cannot lose sight of the kingdom and the church's role in God's grand plan for the world.

For the church on earth to look like Heaven, there are certain dispositions we have to rid our minds of. We must start looking at people through the eyes of God and act like the kingdom we belong to. As believers in the teachings of Christ, we are one big family awaiting our Father's return or our soul's crossover to Heaven, where we all get to share the same citizenship status. There are no majorities or minorities in Heaven, just children of God. We are bought by the same Savior, for the same kingdom, and at the same price.

KEEP THE LIGHT ON

"Again, Jesus spoke to them, saying, "I am the light of the world. Whoever follows me will not walk in darkness but will have the light of life." John 8:12

It's not fun to shut down electricity without an alternative to power your home, cook your food, or see at night. Growing up in Africa, I experienced many blackouts. I've even had a few in the US, especially when we lived in hurricane-prone Florida. No matter how often you go through it, it's never pleasant.

I was listening to Pastor David Jeremiah talk about darkness, and he said darkness cannot be defined without light because darkness is "The absence of light." That is profound! It means darkness can't exist in the presence of light. It can't be defined without it, and it won't even try to show up where light dwells. The power of light cancels out the menace and confusion that darkness brings. John 1:5

states, *"...and the Light shineth in darkness, and the darkness comprehended it not."*

Darkness cowers at the presence of light because the darkness has no power until the light is turned off. To abide in Christ is to live in constant light, and when you live in the light, you will not have to worry about darkness because it dares not to show up at the dominion of light. It is a red-lettered promise by Jesus that whoever follows Him will not walk in darkness because He is the light of the world. Unlike the light switch in our homes that can succumb to power outages, the light from walking with God never goes out because it never bows to worldly elements.

Without the light of Heaven shining through God's children, the world would be consumed by darkness. Speaking to the Jews in the book of Acts 13:47, Paul and Barnabas said, *"For this is what the Lord has commanded us: 'I have made you a light for the Gentiles, that you may bring salvation to the ends of the earth."* Despite the resistance and opposition they experienced, Paul and Barnabas lived in the reality of who they were as lights that reflected whom they served—Christ. Like them, we are the light of the world; if our light stays on, darkness will flee, and the gates of hell will not prevail over us. Although He made sure to remind us to be aware of lurking darkness, Christ compels us to live in the light.

Keep your light on and put darkness out of business in your life. Let heaven be your standard and the kingdom your goal. Watch, pray, and live in the fullness of God's grace.

THROUGH THE DARK VALLEY

"Even though I walk through the darkest valley, I will fear no evil, for you are with me; your rod and your staff, they comfort me." Psalm 23:4

There are many misconceptions about the Christian faith, one of which is the notion that our salvation in Christ prevents us from walking through tough times. The false message paints a picture of a life that limits God's presence to giving us material gains and life's pleasures. It's a belief system ingrained in many Christians, causing them to question their faith when facing challenges.

David is regarded as a man after God's heart. He had amazing adventures walking with God; he was God's friend, and he loved and trusted God. He slayed a giant, killed a lion, and was promoted from a shepherd boy to rule the greatest nation. Yet, despite all his accolades, he was as broken as we are and faced challenges that overwhelmed him just as we do.

I remember one night, my dad had to move my mom to the hospital. As a little girl, I sat there and wondered why a woman who trusted God enough to pray for others would suffer from any sickness. My little mind could not understand how she could be so sure that God could heal anyone while she was dealing with an exhausting ailment.

Looking back, I understand better after walking through many valleys with God. We are not promised the absence of dark valleys; we are promised God's bright, beautiful, and glorious presence. David could have said, "Because you are with me, I will not walk through the valley," but he did not. He said, *"**Though I walk** through the valley, I fear no evil, for you are with me."* It is not the absence of the valley that matters; it is the presence of God that makes the difference.

When I think about my mother, my best example of what it means to be a Christian, I know that walking with God does not mean I get a pass to avoid every bump on the road. It simply means I get to walk with God through the bumps on the road and trust Him to lift me above them. It means I have God by me as I go through any grim time in my life, and I have His shoulder to lean on. Because of my faith in Christ, I have the God of the universe to carry me when I cannot take the next step and to light my path through any dark valley.

WHAT DO YOU HAVE TO LOSE?

"What is more, I consider everything a loss because of the surpassing worth of knowing Christ Jesus my Lord, for whose sake I have lost all things. I consider them garbage, that I may gain Christ and be found in him..." Philippians 3:8-9

Have you ever traded one car to buy another one or transferred one home's equity to live in a different one? The change might stem from the need for something newer, bigger, smaller, more expensive, or cheaper. Whatever the reason, there's always a motivation behind the decision to trade one thing for another. Regardless of the reason, a reward must be attached to the decision.

God is the only essence that completes us and the force that puts our life in order. We can't trade Him for anything. If He offers us everything pertaining to life and godliness, what do we have to lose following Him? Is it the inconvenience of spending a few minutes daily to acknowledge Him before we start the day, gathering with other believers, or identifying as a Christian? Should we abandon the hope of Heaven for the uncertainty of the world we live in or trade good for evil? Nothing can replace God because He completes us; everything else is worthless without Him.

To realize what you stand to gain by following God, think of what you stand to lose, and you will see that without God, life is empty. Money cannot fill the void, fame cannot, and all the power in the world cannot. Paul said, *"I consider everything a loss because of the surpassing worth of knowing Christ."* No pleasure can compare to the satisfaction of being at peace with Christ. No sin is enticing to the extent of reducing the efficacy of the cross, and no life is longer than eternity. No matter what we try to fill our world with, we can never be satisfied until we let God in it.

God's love is deeper than anyone can ever reach, and the peace we know when we place our hands in His can never be matched by anything else. His presence nourishes our lives; in Him, we live, move, and have our being. Although it might come with storms and detours, when God rules your world, your victory is sure.

STEPPING OUT OF THE SHALLOW WATERS

"Deep calls to deep in the roar of your waterfalls; all your waves and breakers have swept over me."
Psalm 42:7

I've watched different series on gold hunting for both land and sea, and the tasks are not for the faint-hearted. I am not a treasure hunter by any means, but I believe that the deeper you dig, the better your chances of finding priceless treasures. I also believe the best diamonds are not sourced from the earth's surface but are buried deep within caves and have to be dug out. It takes more than a kitchen knife to reach the finest diamonds and much more than fishing in the reef to get a priceless pearl.

Growing in our walk with God requires digging deeper so He can continue to unveil Himself to us. It demands surrendering, allowing God to take you to realms you never thought possible, and making His unsearchable mysteries plain to you. It is beyond raising your hand to give God a high five on Sunday morning and waving goodbye at the door after church service.

There is more to walking with God than the few goodies you get in the shallow waters. The more you dig, the better it is. It may require a little more time for bible study, prayer, and growing with other believers. Stepping out of the shallow waters demands that we abandon our will for the Father's will and lay down all our desires at the feet of Christ.

Psalm 42 reflects what most Christians experience in life. Our eternity is in Heaven, but we are not excused from the emotions that come with being humans. God remains the only refuge in a world where it seems impossible to walk through life without thorns thrown on your path with each step. Although it may be painful to get deeper, the rewards you get from following God are unmatched.

Deep calls to deep, and our desire to know God more urges us out of the shallow waters and into the deep. It urges us to leave our worries of getting wet behind and immerse ourselves heart-deep in the things of God. Beyond the reef of life, there are mysteries to unveil and treasures beneath the waves. The deeper we go with God, the clearer life becomes, and we can reach all the treasures of life and godliness when we ride on our Savior's back.

BLESSING IN THE RAIN

"For as the rain comes down, and the snow from heaven, and do not return there, But water the earth, and make it bring forth and bud, that it may give seed to the Sower and bread to the eater."
Isaiah 55:10

There is so much beauty in flowers! I believe they are one of our world's most fabulous creations, and I love surrounding myself with them. I love the colors they add to life and the calm and warmth that comes with each view. But to bud and flourish, flowers need both the cooling of water and the sun's warmth, and most flowers cannot survive without both.

It had been raining through the night, and as I stepped out of my house, I saw the bushes of Mum's flowers outside the door, looking tired and droopy. At first glance, it is easy to assume they are dead and should be trashed. Knowing a few things about flowers, I knew the rain had nourished them and that they only needed the sun to shine on them to maximize the blessing of the rain so they could bloom brightly again.

Before the beauty of the sunshine on the buds of a flower, there must be mud in the root. While there is so much blessing in the rain, it comes with a cloud, and when we go through a rainy season, the weight might overwhelm us and leave us tired. However, if we are rooted in Christ, He will hold us up.

Maybe all you can feel right now are the sting and the weight of the rain; remember that God is doing something inside you through it. He is setting you up for the sunny days ahead because He knows that if you are only exposed to the sunshine of life, you will dry up, and your roots will rot. The people looking at you might think you are not worth much or rule you out of the game of life. They can conclude that the glory of God over you will never shine again. However, your story is not over because the blessing in the rain is reaching your roots to nourish you, and when the sun shines on you, they will see you bloom again.

TRANSCENDING PEACE IN CHRIST

Do not be anxious about anything, but in every situation, by prayer and petition, with thanksgiving, present your requests to God. And the peace of God, which transcends all understanding, will guard your hearts and your minds in Christ Jesus. Philippians 4:6-7

I woke up in the middle of the night with my mind running through the many questions I needed answers to. As I tossed from one side of my bed to the other, trying to find the perfect position to help me sleep, I heard the worship playing softly in my room, and a smile crept up my face. Although I did not hear a loud roar to calm my raging storm, I was conscious of the presence of my Father, and I knew I was not alone.

I have had many of such nights in life, swimming through seas I thought might drown me, walking through roads I thought had no end, and fighting giants I thought would crush me. But somehow, during those moments, the peace I enjoy comes from knowing that God is with me. His presence makes a difference in my response to every situation and challenge I experience. The consciousness of His presence gives me the strength to keep moving.

It is no news that peace has eluded our world, and everyone is just trying to muzzle up the beasts of fear and worry. From challenges within our homes to the ones beyond our borders, there is always something stretching our rest. The peace of God is a refuge. It guards and protects us from surrendering to the opposition. When He prayed for the Philippians, Paul knew that the peace that transcends understanding guards their hearts and minds in Christ Jesus.

Like you, I still have many unanswered questions and will always do until I cross to the other side of life. I do not need to know what tomorrow will look like when I have the author and finisher of my faith as my guide. With God by my side, I enjoy constant peace that calms the raging sea and breaks through the darkest nights.

The peace that transcends understanding comes from walking with God and knowing that as His child, although you will have burdens laid on you in life, you can lay them all back at the feet of Christ. In Him, we have peace that money or fame cannot buy. You do not have to fake it till you make it or live your life weighed down by everything you cannot control because God has the answer to all questions. He knows the end before the beginning, and His peace speaks louder than your worries.

SAFE IN HIS HANDS

"So do not fear, for I am with you; do not be dismayed, for I am your God. I will strengthen you and help you; I will uphold you with my righteous right hand." Isaiah 41:10

Although God's love runs deeper than any mother's love, we are like newborns in God's hands. He is tenderhearted towards humanity; no matter how far we walk away from Him, He keeps coming after us. God is a steadfast refuge and our shield from the scorching elements of life. He doesn't break His hold on you just because you miss your mark, and whichever way the tide leads you, He is there to uphold you.

As extensions of God's character, we understand the tip of the depth of His love through how we respond to a newborn child's needs. Though precious, they are fragile and dependent on adults to care for them. Their beauty and cuteness overshadow the mess of taking care of them. In the same way, God's love covers us. Despite all the messes and imperfections from navigating life, we are precious in His sight.

While we will still feel discomfort as we walk through life, it does not indicate God's absence because He never leaves. He holds us through life's ups and downs and rides on every train we hop on. He is committed to lifting us from all falls and responding to our cries for help. When a child lifts his/her hands to the mother, it symbolizes surrender— "I need you!" Also, when we accept God's love and surrender our will to Him, He trades our fear for faith and weakness for His strength. No matter the corners life pushes us to, we are always safe in God's hands.

There is no better place to be than in the hands of God. I would rather fall in His hands than stand on the pedestal of man, and I would rather live in the circle of God's grace than the million-ton fortress of man's making. I will joyfully rely on God's daily bread than the bounty of a man's silo. I will submit as a servant in the court of Christ rather than be the master of my castle. I will remain a child of God rather than an heir to all earthly thrones, and I would rather be chastised by God than praised by man.

BEYOND WHAT YOU CAN SEE

When the children of Gad and the children of Reuben saw the land of Jazer in Numbers 32, they were ready to abandon God's promise for them and settle there. All they could see was how well their cattle would thrive on that land, and it blinded them from seeing beyond the grazing grass. They told Moses in verse 5, *"Let this land be given unto us for a possession and bring us not into the land of Jordan."*

Humans are limited by what they can see and how far their minds can comprehend. Many of us have settled in Jazer when God's intent for us is Jordan. Just because of the immediate gain we experience, we abandon the infinite abundance that flows from walking with God. We are quick to pull away from holding on to the glorious plans He has for us and embrace a fragment of what should be whole.

God's perspective is wider than ours and reaches beyond our blind spots. His perspective is total and all-encompassing. He can see our beginning before it starts and knows our end from where we are. God knows that just because the grass is green today does not mean it will be green tomorrow. His intent for us is perfect, and we can never go wrong following Him.

I have opted to pitch my tent at different 'Jazers' in my life. I tell God, "Just leave me here, and you go ahead." At different moments in my life, I have experienced momentary pleasure that clouded the fullness and constant peace that comes from following God and allowing Him to chart my path through life. I lay down my sword and submit to the pleasures of the moment instead of staying the course and enjoying the gains of fighting by God. Although He has never led me astray, I hesitate sometimes when He tells me to pack my tent and move on.

Just like the children of Israel, God might have conquered Jazer for us, but it does not mean it is our resting place. Jazer is one of many paths that lead to Jordan, and as long as we walk with God, we will have a better destiny ahead of us. Also, despite the happiness and comfort we feel at the place God wants us to move from, it can never compare to where He is taking us. Do not stop moving on the journey with God because there are many more lands to conquer and a promised land to reach.

WALKING THROUGH THE KING'S HIGHWAY

"God is not a man, that he should lie; neither the son of man, that he should repent: hath he said, and shall he not do it? or hath he spoken, and shall he not make it good?" Numbers 23:19

W hen the Israelites reached Kadesh, they had to pass through Edom to continue their journey to the promised land. Knowing the danger of walking through the city without permission, Moses sent a message to the king. He pleaded with him in Numbers 20:17, *"Please let us pass through your country. We will not go through any field or vineyard or drink water from any well. We will travel along the King's Highway and not turn to the right or the left until we have passed through your territory."* However, despite the promise not to touch or do anything, the Israelites' request to walk through Edom was denied, and an army came against them.

We have all reached our Kadesh at some point in life—a place where God's promises for our life seem like just an Edom away from our reach. Although we can almost glimpse the promised land, we have an army standing between us and walking through the king's highway to th promised land. Despite all efforts to tiptoe around the menacing opposition to our destiny, Edom stands as a barrier between us and getting to our destiny.

I can imagine what was going through Moses' mind and the perplexity of the situation. He had just gotten over the scarcity of water and bickering of the children of Israel, and now this! After all, God made them the promise, and he was only following God and trusting Him to get them to the promised land. Why can't God fight off the army of Edom as He did with the army of Egypt? Why can't He plague the city's people as He did the Egyptians?

Like the Israelites, it is easy to doubt the efficacy of God's promise when we reach our Kadesh, and we might even plead with the enemy to help us pass through a road not on God's map for the journey. Because we can see the King's Highway ahead of us, our short-sightedness will want the shortcut to where God is leading us, wishing God would do more to crush the opposition. Nevertheless, God always waits for us to accept the route He has designated for us, as He is committed to getting us to where He leads us.

Heaven stamps God's promises, and no Edom can stop them. Everything God said He would do, He would do. Just because the King's Highway looks like a faster route to where He is leading us does not mean we will never make it if we do not go through it. Regardless of the army that stands between you and your destiny, God has a better plan for you to get there. Edom is not the end of your story; it is just a chapter, and the Almighty stands strong before you to guide you to the promised land.

THESE ARE MY PEOPLE

"Behold, how good and how pleasant it is for brethren to dwell together in unity! It is like precious ointment... Psalm 133:1-2a

A I saw the text with Jen's name on it, and my spirit leaped because although I had not seen her in four years, her family was an integral part of my life. We spent two years in the same church group, learning, laughing, praying, and camping together. We have moved to a different state, and our families attend different churches now, but the bond between us is Jesus, who is strong enough to defy all odds.

One of the greatest blessings of my faith is sharing life with others who also walk with God. My closest relationships are with those with whom I share the hope of Heaven. The root of the love that bonds the Christian family is deeper than the world can upturn. Even when separated by time or geography, an unbreakable bond keeps us close.

Christ left us a perfect example of what our view of Christianity should look like. His disciples were a bunch of misfits, yet He loved them and shared life with them. When He set out to choose the twelve disciples, He did not look for perfect people, as the Scribes and Pharisees would have. His disciples were rough around the edges and would not pass our definition of 'Worthy.' Peter was impatient, Matthew was an untrusted tax collector, Simon was a zealot, Thomas was skeptical, and Judas was crookedly ambitious.

The pages of the scriptures measure the value system of Christianity and not the colors of our skin, geography, or earthly affluence. Whatever we have here is temporal, and when we walk through the gates of Heaven, the people we will look for are those we have shared our faith with here on earth: blood family or church family—group members, choir mates, prayer partners, and others we have walked the line of faith with. We are more than the definition and label the world places on us because we walk in the fullness of Christ's love for us. He said in John 13:34-35, *"A new command I give you: Love one another. As I have loved you, so you must love one another. By this, everyone will know that you are my disciples..."*

Many Christians miss the beauty of the fellowship of faith because they've subscribed to the division the world throws at us, clouding Christ's clear intent for His Church. Through salvation, we are adopted into the family of God, and our lives become a little brighter when we spend time with other believers. Our faith is rooted in Jesus, the firstborn of the Church, and regardless of our differences, we are bought at the same price by the same savior and heading to the same kingdom.

PART V

JUST BECAUSE I CAN

"But his delight is in the law of the Lord, and in his law doth he meditate day and night." Psalm 1:2

I did not like how the clerk answered me, and in that split second of my heart's response, I was more conscious of how to match her sarcasm with mine. I blurted out the sharp answer before I had a prick in my heart. The Holy Spirit convinced me that I should know better. I am a child of God, and sarcasm should not affect me the way I allow her words to get to me. Despite my displeasure, I immediately turned the table and continued the conversation more cordially.

Although some might argue that I have a right to respond wit-for-wit when I am being disrespected, walking with God should always make me conscious of my Father's presence and honor Him. I do not have to succumb to my pride in moments of discomfort and misrepresent my faith. I am a child of God and belong to a kingdom operating under different rules. My delight is in the law of the Lord, and my greatest desire should be to please Him.

So many of us are living our lives in ways that are more appealing to us than to God. We have prioritized "Self-declared" thrones of importance that we forget the essence of our existence. Our actions and reactions should align with the message of the life, death, and resurrection of Jesus. We should treat people better than we do, listen more than we do, help more than we do, and perhaps endure discomfort more than we do before we give up. No matter what we face here on earth, it cannot be compared to what Christ went through to save us from condemnation.

Until we cross that thin line between life and death, pleasing the flesh will always be at odds with pleasing God, and what we feed more wins more. We should not respond to things based on our flesh's demand but on how God wants us to. Just because we can does not mean we should. Check with Heaven's script before you flip to the next chapter because our hearts' desires can only be measured on Heaven's scale when it continuously seeks to honor God.

THE CULTURED CHURCH

"So, in Christ, we, though many, form one body, and each member belongs to all the others." Romans 12:5

The polarization in our world is overwhelming, and the language is overly divisive. In place of unity, people are divided and thrown into battle arenas, grouped as black, grey, white, majority, minority, rich, and poor. Our differences are magnified, and our joint venture of humanity is suppressed under the demands of racial and cultural identity. The wholeness for which we are all created by God is fractured into nonessentials. When you think you have found the niche to hang on to, you realize there are tinier fragments and that you need to realign.

The message of the cross is different in every way. It is unifying because there are no factions in heaven, and there should be none in the church. God delights in all His children, and we should not act differently when Christians who do not look like us walk through the doors of our church because our focus is to bring "All" to the knowledge of Christ (1Timothy 2:4). It is acceptable when the worship team does look like most people in the room because it is not about us but about glorifying God. The church should reflect Heaven; if that is where we are headed, we must start getting used to sharing the path leading to Heaven with others.

The cultured church is not defined by race. She is the reflection of Heaven. Our identity is rooted in our faith in the Lord Jesus, and when we walk through the doors of any church standing on the truth of God's word, it should feel like home. It doesn't matter what the people look like or what the predominant culture in the building is; it just matters who they follow. And if they proclaim Christ as Lord and honor His commandments, they are family.

The Christ factor in Christendom eliminates the fractures that divide the world. Jesus's blood removes the wedges between us, and His crucifixion and resurrection unify us. As followers of Christ's divine nature, our culture mimics the nature of our Father and our eternal home—Heaven. Though we are many, we are one body! We chant for the same cause and walk the same path with the same hope of the glory of standing before our Savior.

AS YOUR SOUL PROSPERS

"Beloved, I pray that you may prosper in all things and be in health, just as your soul prospers." 3 John 2

I have heard and read so many messages on prosperity, and while some align with God's will for His children, many miss the mark by portraying a view that does not speak to the prosperity of our souls. There is so much focus on how well God wants us to live here on earth that we forget why Christ truly died. His death was more than a meal ticket or healed wound for us. He died to restore our souls to God so we could have abundant life and spend eternity with Him.

The disconnection in Eden separated man from God, but it did not stop God from healing the sick and blessing His people; and it does not stop Him from doing the same today. Before the birth of Christ, God's children enjoyed earthly blessings. Deuteronomy 30:9 says, *"Then the Lord your God will make you most prosperous in all the work of your hands and the fruit of your womb, the young of your livestock and the crops of your land. The Lord will again delight in you and make you prosperous, just as he delighted in your ancestors."*

However, since the fall of Adam and Eve, man has been searching for the perfect peace that comes only from walking with God. A longing that is ingrained in the fabric of humanity to enjoy the garden chats of Eden with our creator. Regardless of what He blesses us with, there is always a quest for more. We desire more kingdoms to rule and more gold to adorn ourselves with in place of our communion with God.

If all we seek or spend our lives chasing after as believers is wealth and physical healing, we will miss the bounty of the prosperity of our souls. However, for the salvation of our souls, Christ had to abandon His majesty, suffer at the hands of His creations, and be crucified on the cross. As the Yahweh, He leveled the walls of Jericho, conquered nations that rose against His people, parted a raging sea, caused a fire to fall from Heaven, and provided for the Israelites in the wilderness.

John says, *"Even as your souls prosper."* Being blessed with earthly things is part of our inheritance but it is only the tip of God's intent for our salvation. Yes, He wants us to prosper, but we can only truly flourish when our souls prosper first. God wants us to enjoy our reconnection to Him through Christ's life, death, and resurrection. He wants our lives to reflect the beauty of Heaven, that even when we pass through the muddy waters of life, we will still be symbols of the true prosperity of Heaven's splendor.

A GLIMPSE OF HEAVEN

"After these things, I looked, and this is what I saw: a vast multitude which no one could count, [gathered] from every nation and all the tribes and peoples and languages [of the earth], standing before the throne and before the Lamb (Christ), dressed in white robes, with palm branches in their hands;" Revelation 7:9

As I walked into the room that evening, I was flushed with the feeling of what Heaven looks like. It was the hundredth anniversary of my church in a few days, and choir members from past and present gathered in the choir room to rehearse for the event. It was the first time I met most of the people in the room because many traveled from other parts of the country for the event. But somehow, I felt I'd known everyone all my life.

We all looked different: old, young, Black, White, Hispanic, male, female, long-haired, and short-haired. However, regardless of all the differences, there was an undeniable sense of kindred spirit in the room. We were gathered for one reason: to glorify our Savior, the Lord Jesus.

Sitting in the corner of the room and singing with all those people left a mark on my heart. It makes me long for the day I will walk through the gates of Heaven. I will not be the new kid on the block or the Nigerian American in the room. I would be home!

The longing for Heaven and standing in God's presence is the most comforting feeling anyone can have. You can live in a house that spans acres and extends to the end of the ocean, but it can never compare to standing on the shores of Heaven. It's a crossover from death to eternal life, shame to glory, rot to incorruptible, and uproar to tranquility.

Some individuals I shared the altar with that weekend are now with Jesus. They've joined the angels to worship at the throne of God. Like the saints before them, they've crossed the line between mortality and eternity, and their salvation in Christ has earned them a right to Heaven. I can imagine their reaction as they walked through the gate because, on an evening not long ago, I also got a glimpse of Heaven as I walked into a room I shared with them.

WHERE ARE YOU GOING?

"There is a way that seems right to a man, but its end is the way of death." Proverbs 14:12

If you ask most motorists on the highway about their destination, they will probably give you the specific place they intend to stop. Hardly will you find anyone driving without a defined destination. Even if they have never been to their intended destination before, they drive with the intent to arrive at their destination for a specific reason.

I have moved a few times in my life, and it is always a challenge to navigate my new neighborhood. While it is always inconvenient, I must figure out the best routes to church, the grocery store, and other places essential for my family to thrive in our new community. The most challenging thing is driving the kids somewhere without knowing exactly where they are going. The first minute you make a turn to an unknown road, they are restless. Until they understand and become familiar with our neighborhood's buildings and other landmarks, they will keep asking, "Where are we going?"

Life is a journey that starts without your consent, but it depends on your choice to accept or reject Christ to determine where the journey ends. However, most of us are driving through life without clearly understanding where we are heading. We are moving in the shadows of other people, not asking ourselves whether today's choices will lead us to divine eternity.

No one joins the driveway and follows other motorists without a defined destination in mind. Suppose everyone around you is heading towards the out-of-order road; if you know it leads to a sharp drop, you will not follow just because it's crowd-approved. You get to choose where your life ends, and it deserves a deep mental dive to make the right choice. You either hand it over to Jesus or follow the world's flow. Either way, there is life beyond whatever we can attain in our mortal state. We can lock our destination to Heaven's gate now before we reach eternal oblivion.

TREASURE IN THE MESS

"And they crucified Him and parted His garments, casting lots, that it might be fulfilled which was spoken by the prophet: "They parted My garments among them, and upon My vesture did they cast lots."
Matthew 27:35

A a few days back, I was watching one of my favorite TV shows and saw someone pay $100,000.00 for a book because of its age and edition. I have seen Americans pay ridiculous money for things on that show, but the love for antiques and memorabilia extends beyond the shores of America. People enter bidding wars over things others will ignore as trash because they are linked to famous humans whom they have probably never met. The longer they have been dead, the more the worth of things linked to them.

Eternity is not prioritized in our value scale, and physical things have gained prominence over things of eternal worth. It never ceases to amaze me to see how much people are willing to pay for some old furniture or jewelry just because of reasons within the curtains of life. Some have died in their quest to follow a map that leads to a hiddent treasure. To a layman, the cross on which Jesus died is worth more than His actual death, and the thorn He wore would be the world's greatest treasure to the finest archeologist.

We are limited by our understanding of what we can see and touch, and they block our minds from grasping the joy that comes from walking with and seeing things from God's perspective. For instance, the greatest occurrence the world has ever witnessed is not the creation of the highest mountain, the deepest sea, or even the creation of man. The greatest occurrence in human history is the birth, death, and resurrection of Christ, yet our minds reduced the moment He was crucified to casting lots over who gets His blood-soaked garment.

The world is a mess, and God is the greatest treasure we can find in it. He knows it all and owns it all. It is easy for us to get caught up in things of less value to eternity and forget that accepting the gift of salvation offered by Christ is greater than winning a bidding war on His garment.

BALANCING LIFE ON CHRIST'S FIRM FOUNDATION

"Therefore, the Lord God said: "Look, I have laid a stone in Zion, a tested stone, a precious cornerstone, a sure foundation; the one who believes will be unshakable." Isaiah 28:16

L ife is like a balancing act. We each live like circus performers trying to walk from one end of a suspended rope to another. Our hands are stretched, trying to travel a distance on a plank placed on a rolling ball. A simple distraction can send you flying in the air or down a spiral fall, and no matter how firmly you hold the balance stick, you need all your senses to make it to the finish line.

To say we live in an unstable world is putting it mildly. Even if you get your personal life under control, you are surrounded by so much confusion and uncertainty that it places you back in the bubble. Two fractions can't even agree on right and wrong, and the laws governing our daily living are shaky and dependent on who's at the helm of affairs.

Like most people, I thought I had my life figured out and Christ only needed to take a back seat. However, as I grew in my walk with Him, I realized that it was safer for me to switch roles and let Him do the driving while I rode along. That way, I know that when I get in a jam, He'll help me.

While certain laws of life are constant, there is so much nitty-gritty beyond our control. You might get the best education and still struggle to keep your bank flowing with cash. You might marry the perfect man or woman and keep fighting for your marriage to stay afloat. You can raise your children in church and still deal with a prodigal child. There are just so many parts to keeping your balance that it takes God for you to stay stable.

Being a child of God sets you apart; it gives you a soft landing on the solid rock of Christ. He is the firm foundation for any life, the rock of ages, and the essence of our existence. Although being a Christian does not get you off the balancing act of life, it affirms your safety as you walk through the tightrope. Even when you fall, your father will catch you before you reach the ground.

FULLY AND TOTALLY LOVED BY GOD

"But as many as received Him, to them gave He the power to become the sons of God, even to those who believe in His name." John 1:12

Before I had my first child, I could not fully grasp how much my mother loved me. I did not understand that her love was built so strong that it mimics the love of God for His children. There were six of us, but we were loved equally by a mother who would gladly give herself up for each of us.

When it was just my daughter, it was easy to give her full attention from the moment she joined our small family. I could not have imagined the possibility of loving another child as much as I loved her. I thought nothing was left in my love reservoir and I would have to divide my love with her brothers. I expected the dynamics to shift as we welcomed two new children. However, I was amazed by how easy it was to love each of them fully and totally.

Despite their differences, it was natural to fall in love with my second child and then the third.

As my children grew, my love for them remained steadfast, along with the beauty and messes that come with that. It is not measurable and defies time and space. No matter how far they are from me, I love them as much as I would if they were right by me. Also, no matter the attention one of them demands, per time, my heart is constantly fully engaged with the other two.

To be called a child of God is the best title anyone can have. It sets us apart and puts us in a class like no other. God loves us fully and totally, beyond space and time. No matter how far we are from Him, we are loved by our heavenly Father with everlasting love. Just like every child fills a godly mother's heart, we fill God's heart. He is committed to nurturing, correcting, and helping us find our way as we grow in Him. God does not get so busy with one child and forgets the other because we are ingrained in the palm of His hands (Isaiah 49:16).

Understanding God's love is the greatest discovery any man can make. It liberates us from the desire to please anyone but Him and sets us free from participating in the devil's blame game. No longer are we subject to the remnants from the Father's table but we are partakers of the family feast.

STAIRWAYS TO HEAVEN'S GATE

"So do not fear, for I am with you; do not be dismayed, for I am your God. I will strengthen you and help you; I will uphold you with my righteous right hand." Isaiah 41:10

Walking through life comes with difficulties. It is a journey through a maze of unknowns, and no matter how well we think we have figured it out, it always throws something new at us. It is a journey that starts with birth but does not end in death because death leads to eternity.

For me, the journey to Heaven is like climbing steep stairs to a mountaintop because we live in an imperfect world where we must contend with the raging waves of life and the constant battle of our minds. As I walk up those stairs, there are times I have enough strength to run toward the mountaintop, and there are times I get too weary to take one step. In every moment, all that matters is that I am not looking back to where I left before Christ saved me and that, although I might not be a step closer, I remind myself of how close Heaven is to me.

Like everyone who has been and is still walking through the stairs of life, I have enjoyed so many things in my life, and I have also been through some dark roads and painful turns. Regardless of the condition of each turn, the only reason I am still standing is that I am not walking alone. I have placed my hands in the hands of Christ and entrusted my life to Him. If I am running, He is right beside me, and when I am too weak to take a step, He is right there, stroking my back until I am rested enough to continue my journey.

God is not a taskmaster, expecting you to "suck it up" and move on. He is the comforter who will stand by you until you are ready to keep moving. He is not disappointed by your weakness because His strength is made perfect in your weakness. Your heavenly Father is not repulsed by the wounds you sustain through life because He holds the balm of Gilead. He is not weary of your tears because He will wipe each drop away, no matter how long they flow. To the saved, Jesus is a friend that sticks closer than a brother and the only constant in our inconsistent life.

THE LORD'S PORTION

"For the Lord's portion is his people…"
Deuteronomy 32:9a

The majestic view of the ocean from the hotel window was captivating. I could hardly look away from the waves rising and falling and the sea of white sands. It was so beautiful and mesmerizing to watch the endless blue water that commands so much power yet makes life seem easier. My few days of vacation were almost over, but the majesty of the ocean will stay with me forever.

I love the ocean, the mountains, and all the things that remind me of God's greatness and creative ability. How can something so massive and endless as the ocean be perfectly separated from land? How are the *Iroko* trees formed, and how are the mountains carved with such details? When we think about all the planets, galaxies, and billions of stars that light up our world every night, there is sobering awe for the God behind it all.

The twenty-four elders in Revelations 4:11 said, *"Thou art worthy, O Lord, to receive glory and honor and power; for Thou hast created all things, and for Thy pleasure, they are and were created."* You can argue about His existence, but He speaks through the seas' waves, the rain's trickle, and the wind's rustle.

Despite the unfathomable awe of all of God's creation, the Lord's portion is His people, and He delights in us. Of all His majestic creations, humanity holds a special place in the heart of the Father. A billion sparkles in the sky and the loudest roars of the sea are no match for the teardrops of a man or woman walking with God. His love for His children is infinite, and His commitment to them is everlasting.

Man is extraordinary, created by God, in God's image, and for God's glory. The shooting stars or blazing sun cannot compare to the intricacies of the god-like man. The Psalmist says, *"Know ye that the Lord, He is God; it is He that hath made us, and not we ourselves. We are His people and the sheep of His pasture."* Psalm 100:3.

CALL ME "CHRISTIAN!"

"So, for a whole year, Barnabas and Saul met with the church and taught great numbers of people. The disciples were called Christians first at Antioch."
Acts 11:26

When people called the disciples Christian in Antioch, it was because they looked, talked, and behaved like Christ. It simply means "Christ-like." When Christ walked on earth, His focus was Heaven, and His purpose was to restore man to God. Because we share His identity, our focus must be on Heaven, and our primary drive in life should be to attract the world to Him. Christ's love was absolute, and despite the thrills and pulls of the world, He did not miss His mark.

Being a Christian comes with a great sense of responsibility to the kingdom we represent. It means we heed the call of Paul in Philippians 2:5-11 to adopt the mindset of Christ. He writes in verse 5, *"Let this mind be in you, which was also in Christ Jesus."* Although the world was totally different from the Kingdom He came from, Jesus was not swayed by the "acceptables" of His time. He lived righteously and laid a path for us to follow, having walked it Himself, lining it with rays from Heaven to help us through.

I love my identity with Jesus, and my name says it all— "I AM A CHRISTIAN," which means I bear the likeness of Christ. It is not a name I carry with levity or carelessness. It is the highest honor and dignity mark because it is tied to Christ. With the name, I represent the most privileged group of people to walk the earth, and my entire identity is summed up by it. I do not speak for any group or affiliation other than the scripture and the Lord Jesus. In a world where everyone is expected to pick a side, my choice is constant because I picked mine—once and for all—when I accepted to be called Christian.

As Christians, we follow Heaven's script. Every page and every chapter of our lives should be written by and for God. Our nature is defined by the legacy Christ left for us. Except we look to Him, we will miss the mark because He is the perfect mirror through which our lives should reflect. When we declare, "I am a Christian," it should be enough to show people what Christ lived like when He walked this earth.

THE MORE SYNDROME

"But godliness with contentment is great gain. For we brought nothing into this world, and it is certain we can carry nothing out." 1 Timothy 6:6-7

As I looked through my closet, trying to pick my clothes for the day, I got a little frustrated because although I had so much to choose from, I could not decide fast enough. It was more confusing than comforting to have so much and yet feel the perfect pick is missing. What is it about us that no matter how much we have, we keep adding to it? While there is nothing wrong with enjoying God's blessings in our lives, there should be a check to restrict us from taking our "wanting more" syndrome farther than it should go.

The human heart is ingrained with the quest for more. We want more fame, money, houses, influence, just more and more. Even when we have more than we need, we always desire to add to the bank or fleet of cars in our garage. We fill the closet with shoes we have not worn for months and adorn our lives with momentary gratifications that only last so long.

The power struggle of the world's government systems reinforces the need for us to continue engaging in the battle of the "fittest takes the trophy." Instead of learning from the character of the creator of the universe, humanity is disintegrating to a level so low that we believe it is okay to trample on others to get what we want. Regardless of the acquisition cost, the quest for more reduces the strength of empathy and mercy to the weakness of hate and greed.

Paul writes in Hebrews 13:5, *"Let your conduct be without covetousness; be content with such things as you have."* As followers of Christ, our sufficiency is in God because He is our El Shaddai. When we find rest in Him, He satisfies our longing for more with the fullness of Himself.

Contentment is indeed a "great gain." Through contentment, we enjoy peace because it reminds us there is always someone below the ladder and we are blessed to have as much as we have. Contentment makes us see abundance instead of the need for more. Without it, you might be the richest person on earth and still want something someone else has that your money can't buy.

WHO DO YOU FOLLOW?

"Come, follow me," Jesus said..." Matthew 4:19a

The GPS has revolutionized how we drive. For someone like my husband, it is one of the greatest inventions of all time. Gone are the days when we must use a two-page map or follow a penned list of roads to get to places. Using a phone connected to the internet, we are easily directed in real-time to navigate places we have never been before easily and confidently.

Sometimes, we need alternatives to using our phones for directions because, without an internet connection, we will lose navigation guidance. To be safe, if you are driving through roads with limited internet services, you might want an actual GPS that works regardless of the internet. There are also limitations to trusting a phone or an actual GPS because, for any of them to work, the device must be charged so you don't risk losing your guide.

When Jesus told Peter and Andrew to follow Him in Matthew 4, He did not expect them to have alternatives. It was a simple command that started an amazing relationship between them and Christ. They might have been contented with their lives as fishermen and did not expect Jesus to step into their situation as He did. However, when Jesus came into the picture, they had to leave their comfort zone to trust Him.

Following Christ does not leave us with alternatives because we do not need any. He is enough light for us to walk through the darkest alleys of life and has enough strength to move the heaviest mountains we face. Jesus always gets it right because He is the "Truth" personified. He knows every turn and cracks in our journey. Our burden is light with Him.

So many things are calling on us and diverting our attention, and it is okay to trust the good people in our lives. However, no matter how well we trust them, we are called to follow Christ, not our heart, the crowd, or beloved pastors. Christ alone gets it right a hundred percent of the time, and we need to weigh everything with Him through the filter of His Word. Like the GPS systems, our hearts and other people can run out of batteries and might route us wrongly, but when we follow Jesus, He will always lead us right.

FREEDOM INDEED

"So, if the Son sets you free, you will be free indeed."
John 8:36

My son recently worked on a school project about freedom. When I asked him what freedom meant and where he felt freedom the most, he said 'home.' To him, home means safety, rest, and acceptance. To him, it represents the place of the greatest sense of freedom.

The mention of the word 'home' brings immediate calm to most humans. When we are far from it, we long for it, and regardless of how little we have in it, home is still where we feel the most valued. Home is where we can be everything we are without masking it.

Although we feel the freest in our homes, they must be organized for them to remain habitable. We dedicate different rooms for different purposes, and different appliances are used for different functions. If we misuse one for the other, it becomes an abuse. It is the same with God. He created the world and put things in place to ensure order.

Freedom does not mean we get to do whatever we want with our lives because true freedom comes from total abandonment of our will at the feet of the cross to follow Christ. It is a state of surrendered heart to God's will. Freedom is not the absence of order or the presence of a million different choices. It is giving up all your choices to adopt one—honoring God. True freedom gives a sense of satisfaction and peace from knowing your actions are God-approved and Heaven-backed.

Many of us walk around thinking we can do or say anything in the name of freedom, even if it misrepresents Heaven. Nevertheless, with sin comes bondage. When Jesus was asked in John 8:33b, *"How can you say that we shall be set free?"* He answered them, debunking the notion that sin equals freedom. He said in verse 34, *"Truly, truly, I say to you, everyone who practices sin is a SLAVE to sin."*

Living in sin separates us from the only one who can truly exchange our hearts' greatest longings with genuine freedom. Speaking with my son, I asked him if, just because he is free at home, it would be okay for him to fill a cup with milk and intentionally pour it onto the sofa or use the kitchen instead of the bathroom. He said both would be wrong and nasty. In the same light, just because Christ gave us freedom does not mean we get to misalign the order of life and godliness. While we may occasionally spill dirt and make mistakes because of our mortal imperfections, orderliness in our pursuit of righteousness means we do not live with the dirt.

A DOLLAR FOR A DIAMOND

In a recent conversation with my husband, we weighed the best action on a particular business challenge. We had to make a choice that might cost us just a little more than our initial plan or risk losing so much more if we didn't. When we focused on the immediate, it felt somewhat daunting to add the extra cost, but when we looked beyond the immediate to see the bigger picture, it was wiser to eliminate the unnecessary risk with a few extra bucks per month. Although our decision came at a small cost now, we knew the alternative could cost us thousands more eventually.

Oftentimes, the thought of what we can lose now can cloud what we stand to gain later. We gratify our immediate desires at the expense of the abundant joy of delayed gratification. Like most people, I'm not too fond of the sting of antiseptic when I get a cut. However, instead of enduring a pinch of pain to stop a small bleeding cut, I know if we ignore it, there is the danger of infection and engorgement.

Our life is worth more than the pleasures or pains of today. Although you cannot spend it because the worth is beyond the rough edges, a raw diamond is more valuable than the cleanest, crispiest, shiniest one-dollar note. In the same light, eternity might be a distance away, but it is far more valuable than our existence today.

If we know that the most significant gain is to make Heaven, we must constantly trade our pennies for the matchless riches of following Christ. The hope of spending eternity with Him makes it easier to bear some pain here and there as we journey through life. If we look beyond the immediate discomfort or short-lived delights to think of our faith in God and all the goodies that come with it, we will have the strength to fight another day.

Admonishing us to honor God with how we live, Paul writes in Hebrews 12:2, *"Looking unto Jesus, the author, and finisher of our faith, who for the joy that was set before Him endured the cross, despising the shame and is set down at the right hand of the throne of God."* Our Lord Jesus is a perfect example. Because He died, we live, and because of His obedience, millions of people across time and space get to walk the narrow path leading to God's throne.

PART VI

THE FATHER'S TABLE

"You prepare a table before me..." Psalm 23:5a

Most of the time, the family eats at different times and sometimes in separate parts of the room, but eating together at the dining table is one of my favorite things. It creates the most relaxing atmosphere for us to enjoy meals and laugh together. I love watching the kids' faces and watching them make fun of one another. There is something about it that sets the tone of unity and freedom, and sometimes, I wish it could go on longer because of the memories we make.

Our last born is the newest in the family, and he gets the most attention because he has more to learn about table manners. Until recently, he sat beside me at the dining table because, unlike his brother and sister, he needed help during mealtimes. I help him with simple things like cutting his chicken and pouring his juice while teaching him how to do it himself.

When you surrender your life to Christ and trust Him to be your Lord, He becomes your Father, loving you with everlasting love. He welcomes you into His family and surrounds you with all you need to succeed with Him. He is not irritated by your messes but helps you through the learning process of cleaning up.

A few years back, I was discussing with a group about what diversity should look like in the Christian fold, and I made an example of how God wants us to approach Him and each other. When I serve dinner, all my children have equal rights to eat with the family at the dining table. None of them are guests at the table, and they do not need my or their siblings' permission to sit and eat with the rest of the family. Their birth sealed their right to participate.

Similarly, our right to God's family is sealed by our rebirth in Christ. The Father's table is set for all His children regardless of what they look or sound like. At His table, it does not matter what language you speak or if you are short or tall, black or white, young or old. If you are part of the family, you have an equal right to participate. Regardless of your stage in your walk with Christ, once you cross the line of salvation, you are family.

Like my youngest, the newer you are, the better the seat you get at the table because God knows He might need to help you wipe your sticky hands and clean the mess around you.

THE PATH MY MOMMA WALKED

"Her children rise up and call her blessed; her husband also, and he praises her: 'Many women have done excellently, but you surpass them all."
Proverbs 31:28-29

As I lay sleeping, I could hear her voice whispering softly near me and feel her hand resting gently on my head. This was one of the several nights I was awoken by my mother praying over me. Although I didn't enjoy losing a few minutes of my sleep on nights like that, it was a regular part of my childhood, and I found peace in her tall silhouette towering over me in the dead of night.

Mum was not, by any means, an average woman raising six kids. At every turn, she faced many Goliaths in different forms, but she was a warrior who stood to fight off all of them. She had a firm understanding of who God is and where she stood with Him; as a result, she never backed down from the giants.

Her commanding presence was directly tied to her heavenly Father, and regardless of where the tide pushed her, her focus was fixed on Jesus. Mum woke us up at six every morning and at nine every night to sing hymns and pray together as a family. While I cannot claim that was fun then, looking back, I adore her for her tenacity. Despite the many challenges she faced, through her unwavering love for God, she laid a firm foundation that I cannot imagine walking away from the God she served.

Walking with God is the greatest adventure anyone can embark on in life, and seeing my mother walk that path ahead of me gives me the strength to tread fearlessly on the treacherous terrains of life. I know who I am in Christ because I saw my mum live out the beauty of God's grace and love. Her life did not always look pretty, but her joy never faded because it was rooted in Christ.

In a world where the human identity has become so confusing, and the sense of worth is uncertain, it takes knowing God to know who you are, and I am glad I had a mother who showed me that path. She was devoted to her husband and gave everything up to see her children flourish. My momma was a woman who lived for others, spicing up her world with the joy that only God gives, and she loved overwhelmingly and beyond reproach.

A SPECK OF GLITTER

"Above all else, guard your heart, for everything you do flows from it." Proverbs 4:23

My daughter told me a story someone shared with them at church to reinforce the importance of minding little things before they become big things. She said it started with going to her friend's house for a sleepover. During the sleepover, they had fun playing with glitter. However, they couldn't have imagined such an innocent act would result in an adverse event her family did not plan for.

When she returned home, she noticed her eyes were swollen, but little did she know that the pleasure and beauty of the glitter she played with at her friend's house would send her on a long road of recovery. When the swelling persisted, the parents took her to the hospital and later learned that a speck of glitter had traveled behind her eye and was moving toward her brain. By this time, it was beyond reach, and she had to go through surgery to get the tiny alien in her head out before it got to her brain.

In a world where information is everywhere, we need to sharpen our spiritual sifting skills so that only things that honor God can penetrate our minds and keep out those that can hurt us. Different ideologies fight for our hearts' approval, pulling us from side to side instead of standing firm on the unshakable truth of God's word.

Most people love glitters; I mean, I do. They are shiny and beautiful, but who would have thought that something so pretty could almost damage a little girl's brain? Out of the thousands of tiny glitters she played with that night, one managed to escape to the most dangerous part of her body, causing a major problem and sending her family on a health scare spiral ride.

Allowing a tiny, weightless, negligible worldly glitter to travel in the wrong direction of our mind can render us confused and helpless. Just like a beautiful handful of glitters, it is so easy for us to be swayed by the innocence of little things that can have a lasting effect on our core values as followers of Christ. Little things that make us hide behind the notion of "it does not matter" until it does matter. Yes, we are surrounded by so many thorns prickling our delicate souls, but if we follow the course charted by Jesus, we will avoid being bruised.

DEATH OF ONE, THE SALVATION OF ALL

"Praise be to the God and Father of our Lord Jesus Christ! In His great mercy, he has given us new birth into a living hope through the resurrection of Jesus Christ from the dead and into an inheritance that can never perish, spoil or fade." 1 Peter 1:3-4

Mankind was doomed to the grip of hell when Eve took the first bite from the forbidden fruit and shared it with Adam in the Garden of Eden (Genesis 3:6). At that moment, we were left to wander through the roads of uncertainty to retrieve that which we lost when we were separated from God. Because sin took its toll on the human mind, instead of finding God, we moved farther away from Him.

Since Christ's death and resurrection, the journey to the cross has captured humanity's attention. Imagine knowing that the mission you are embarking on leads to crucifixion for sins you did not commit and payment of the debt you did not owe. Jesus knew exactly what He was getting into when He left Heaven to walk among us. He knew how the story began and ended.

Paul writes in 1 Corinthians 15:3, *"For I delivered to you as of first importance what I also received, that Christ died for our sins according to the Scriptures."* His death was not an occurrence in the moment of weakness but an occurrence in the culmination of love. He was condemned that we might be justified; carried the cross, so our burdens might be light; died that we might live, and by His stripes, we were healed.

As He walked through the streets of Jerusalem with the cross on His shoulder, Jesus's intent was apparent reconciliation of humanity back to God. For our salvation, He gave up His splendor and majesty, subjecting Himself to human treason and ridicule. He carried a cross He did not deserve and died in the hands of those He loved beyond measure.

Despite His sufferings and the extent of the love demonstrated through the crucifixion of Jesus, many are still wandering, looking for answers to questions answered in Golgotha. Yes, God loves us, yes, we can call Him Father again, and yes, we get to spend eternity with Him. 1 Peter 3:18 states, *"For Christ also died for sins once for all, the just for the unjust, so that He might bring us to God, having been put to death in the flesh, but made alive in the spirit."*

THE VALUE OF YOU!

"For thus saith the Lord of hosts......... for he that touch you touch the apple of his eye." Zechariah 2:8

The world is growing colder daily, and people are venting their frustration at others. They project their dissatisfaction on those around them because they do not know the value God places on them. They reduce the worth of people they meet to less than the value God places on them.

Knowing who God is and acknowledging His sovereignty over all things clears our eyes of all the obscurity that limits our view of who we are and how God views us. Proverbs 9:10 says, *"The fear of the Lord is the beginning of wisdom, and knowledge of the Holy One is understanding."* A rich man's son lives conscious of his father's wealth and approaches his needs, considering what the dad can make possible.

David clearly understood who God is, which translated into his understanding of who he is in God. Goliath, or even King Saul, could not reduce his worth because he was confident of the value God placed on him. He declared God's majesty and gave Him preeminence. He said in Psalm 139:14, *"I praise you because I am fearfully and wonderfully made; your works are wonderful; I know that full well."*

When you begin to see yourself according to God's definition of you, a fire lights up in your mind that cannot be quenched by the grime and filthiness of anyone's hate. No one can put a value on you or estimate the cost of all that God has purposed for you to be. You are more significant than the mind of any man or woman, and your worth is extraordinary. You are God's masterpiece, an unbreakable diamond with a price tag worth more than all the money in the world.

You occupy the most delicate part of God, and anyone who touches you touches the apple of His eye. You are perfect, and how God views you is all that counts. Stop selling yourself short of the giant God made you, allowing people to rearrange the chapters of your life and dictate the narrative of a story written by God. You are as rich and flawless as the Lord made you, and you are not a victim until you succumb to the lies you are being told.

AS STRONG AS YOUR WALK WITH GOD

"Even youths grow tired and weary, and young men stumble and fall, but those who hope in the Lord will renew their strength. They will soar on wings like eagles; they will run and not grow weary; they will walk and not be faint." Isaiah 40:30-31

The world measures strength by physical prowess, wealth, fame, and connections. To be accepted, you either look the part or pay the fine. It is instinctively embedded in our humanity to gravitate towards people who seem more put together. If two men walk into a room and one looks strong and well-dressed while the other looks less "impressive," our natural response is to give more attention to the former.

The redemption story does not fit into our worldly expectations in any way. God was intentional in the choices surrounding the birth of Christ. His earthly heritage was anything but glamorous, and although He was "majesty personified" by virtue of His Godhood, He came as the firstborn son of a carpenter from an oppressed group.

One of my favorite stories in the Bible is the story of David and Goliath. It is a great example of how God measures strength and how a man displays unhinged courage in the El Gibbor (God the Almighty). The entire army, including the king, was menaced by a giant because he looked and sounded stronger than everyone. He was so sure no man would dare stand up to him, saying, *"This day, I defy the armies of Israel!"* 1 Samuel 17:10a.

Goliath might be taller than everyone on the battlefield, but a man is as strong and wise as his walk with God. David understood this; although he was not even qualified to fight in the battle against the Philistines because he was too young, he ended the war with a simple slingshot. Unlike the armies of Israel, David was unperturbed by the height or weight of Goliath. He was more upset that Goliath dared to defile the armies of the living God (1 Samuel 17:26).

Despite all the different challenges David faced, including the giant Goliath, he declared in Psalm 28:7, *"The Lord is my strength and my shield."* He was in a league of his own because He walked with God. If you walk with God, you do not have to run faster than everyone or be the most famous in the room because your strength is rooted in the Almighty. As long as you stay focused on Him and continue to pursue His purpose for your life, you are guaranteed victory over the Goliaths on the battlefields of life.

RUN YOUR RACE

"Therefore, we also, since we are surrounded by so great a cloud of witnesses, let us lay aside every weight, and the sin which so easily ensnares us, and let us run with endurance the race that is set before us, looking unto Jesus, the author and finisher of our faith." Hebrews 12:1-2a

I love the Olympics, and Sprint is my favorite game to watch. I love the intensity and excitement leading up to crossing the finish line. Like the other games, it requires endurance and extreme focus because a little mistake can cause a runner the high price of missing Olympic medals.

The demand on the runners can sometimes seem unfair because, after four years of constant practice, they can be disqualified from running in the Olympic race if they miss the whistle by a microsecond. Moments leading to the start of the race require all the runners' senses to be alert and ready to run when the whistle goes off. There is no room for error, and I am guessing that all they can think of in the few seconds before the whistle blows is avoiding a false start.

Paul said in 1 Corinthians 9:26, *"I do not run like someone running aimlessly."* The Christian journey is a race, not a stroll in a park. Just because we have crossed the line of salvation does not mean we lose focus on where we are headed. A goal is set before us, and until we reach Heaven, our entire focus should be on Christ, which is required to help us get to the finish line gloriously. While the Christian race is not to outwit one another, we must remember that we are running for a higher calling.

Many of us are entangled in other people's races instead of focusing on ours. We lose sight of the finish line, looking sideways and backward at things that should not concern us. We would rather criticize others for stumbling than take the time to ensure we do not stumble, too. Instead of lending a helping hand to those who need it, we crisscross other lanes to trip others, forgetting for whom we run—Christ.

If Paul, a man whose life embodied God's grace, thought it necessary to remind himself to focus on His calling, how much more we? There is just too much to lose if we miss the mark and so much to gain if we run the race right. Unless we intend to encourage and help those who find it difficult to continue, there is no time to condemn others.

Christ wants us to succeed, and He left us an example of Himself. He was laser-focused on His mission, and even when they thought He was going to 'magically' end the Roman rule, He knew His journey would lead Him to the cross at the hands of those He came to save. Yet, regardless of all the pain that came with that, He did not lose sight of what He knew He had to do for us to be reconciled to God. Run your race because the success of many is tied to it.

A MILLION MILES WITH JESUS

"As for you, if you walk before me faithfully as David your father did, and do all I command, and observe my decrees and laws, I will establish your royal throne, as I covenanted with David, your father, when I said, 'You shall never fail to have a successor to rule over Israel." 2 Chronicles 7:17-18

I was fifteen when I became a Christian, a high school student with little to worry about and a limited understanding of the world. I knew very little about life then, but what I knew was enough to endear my will to the love of God. Somehow, there was deep assurance that Christ was more committed to me than any relationship I know. Although I had my parents to provide for my needs and take care of me, Jesus brought something to the table that, even at that young age, no one could give me—peace and eternal hope.

Getting on my knees and asking Jesus to be my Lord that afternoon was the first step in a million-mile journey. All I knew was that I would never be alone from that moment. Something changed in me that day because I was no longer abandoned in my teenage whirlwind world, left to figure life out. I had a guide to walk me through the thorny terrains of life and a constant friend to lean on.

The faith journey starts with repentance and total surrender to God's will. It is a journey where Christ is your companion, with endless grace and mercy. He knows where you are coming from and where each turn in your life leads. Even if you miss it, God knows how to reroute you to your spot in destiny and project Heaven's light on your path.

Since I placed my little hands in Christ's mighty hands and trusted Him to lead me, He has never let go. Through the plains, the mountain tops, the valleys, and the hills, He is the sun that shines through the thick clouds and the anchor when the billows roll. I am joyfully resolved that I will walk a million miles, a million years with Jesus, than take a single step without Him.

THAT I MAY KNOW HIM

*"That I may know Him and the power of His
resurrection and the fellowship of His sufferings, being
made conformable unto His death." Philippians 3:10*

Before I met my husband, he was a total stranger to me
and me to him. I didn't even know his name, history, or
dreams about the future. While I believe in first love, I would
not say ours was close to it. If there were a picture of what I
thought my husband would be, he would miss a mark or two.

Over time, I was drawn to him and wanted to know more
about him. I was intrigued by his story and passion for God.
We spent every available time learning about each other's
past and goals for the future. At some point, we both knew
that we love each other and God has plans for us. We agreed
to start a fun and demanding journey. It's been decades since
then, and I know so much more about him today than I did—
the first evening I met him. We are as close as any two
humans can be, and I know him enough now to finish some

of his sentences. However, even with that and three children between us, I am still learning new things about him daily.

Following Christ is not a one-said-and-done deal. It is like a maze that requires knowing His will as we take each step towards the exit sign. It is a continuous process of learning at His feet and getting to know Him better each waking moment of our life. Knowing Christ is a love affair that should never end because, unlike my earthly love, it continues till eternity. As long as we still have our flesh cloak on, we need Him to help us understand what pleases Him.

Writing to the Philippians in chapter 3, Paul emphasizes that following Christ requires a total surrender of our will to please the flesh because the knowledge of who Jesus is liberates us from the hold of worldly longings. He said in verse 10, *"That I may know him, and the power of his resurrection, and the fellowship of his sufferings, being made conformable unto his death."*

We should not fight some battles—particularly when Christ is not in them. However, many of us fight when we should pray or seek peace because we act before we ask. With each new social or political issue, life question, or challenge, we must know how Jesus feels about it and the role He intends us to play before we act. Knowing Christ exceeds the story of the baby in a manger, the man who mentored the twelve disciples, healed the sick, and was unjustly crucified.

Jesus is more than a good guy who graced the earth with perfection. He is God and Lord over all things. To those who are saved, He is a Father who desires that our lives reflect the fellowship of His sufferings and His call for us to live holy. James 2:19 says, *"Thou believes that there is one God; thou doest well: the devils also believe, and tremble."* If Paul, who saw Jesus physically, declares his desire to know Christ more, how much more, you and I.

TUNNELS TO GLORY

"Weeping may tarry for the night, but joy comes with the morning." Psalm 30:5b

It was a long bus ride from Yobe to Lagos, and as I stepped off the bus that afternoon, I was overwhelmed by the journey ahead of me. It was the end of college and the National Youth Service program, the end of the life and routine I had grown accustomed to. There were no more lectures to attend or classmates to study with. No more government monthly allowances or stipends to live on. The world was ahead of me, and I had to face or be drowned by it.

Although I have looked forward to completing college and fulfilling the mandatory program, I wondered what the future holds. What is next? Would I get a job and get married? Would I be able to contribute positively to my world? I had many questions but had no one to ask but myself.

We all go through seasons of uncertainty at different points in life. Times—when we are unsure what the answers to the million questions rambling in our minds would be. Seasons when the dark tunnels feel endless, without hope in sight. It is like a wilderness without trails or paths to follow, and all we can do is hold on to the invisible hands of our Savior and allow Him to guide us through the maze.

When God told Abram to leave his country in Genesis 12 for a land He would show him, one would think that because it was God who called him, the journey would be easy. However, Abram had to go through different tunnels to reach the promised land. He had to contend with the Canaanites, the Egyptians, his nephew, and Sodom and Gomorrah.

As a child of God, your challenges now do not have to consume you. They are just tunnels to glory. Moses went through the wilderness before he became a deliverer; David tended the sheep and fought a Goliath before he became a king; Joseph was betrayed and sold to slavery before he managed the wealth of Egypt; Esther lived in a strange land before she became a queen who saved a nation; and ultimately, our Lord Jesus endured the cross before He redeemed the world.

Today, we call Abraham the father of faith because of his unwavering trust in God. He believed in God, and it was counted onto him for righteousness (Romans 4:3). It is about two decades since I stepped off that bus from Yobe, and looking back, although I have gone through many tunnels since then, I have seen God's glory shine on me at the end of each. He walks with us and cheers when we make it through. No matter how windy and dark the journey may be, it has an end!

WHO DO YOU SAY I AM?

"For by grace are ye saved through faith; and that not of yourselves: it is the gift of God: Not of works, lest any man should boast." Ephesians 2:8-9

I have participated in many Christian conversations that always end with us discussing people's perspectives of Jesus. Regardless of the topic, it is always convenient to shift the focus from ourselves to the inadequacies of others. We embrace the comfort of merely knowing Christ as a good God and disregard the need for us to focus on our walk with Him constantly.

Frequently, Christians are more concerned about what people say about Jesus and how they view His teachings than how we represent Heaven. We easily step away from our joint mission with Christ to call people to repentance and reduce the purpose of our salvation to a platform for condemnation. In place of seeking grace daily, we put ourselves on a pedestal so high that we forget that Heaven's standard of life is way above our human league and that we are simply products of grace through the sufferings of Christ.

In Matthew 16:13-20, the disciples were eager to tell Jesus what others thought of Him when He asked them in verse 13, *"Who do people say I am?"* They told Him that some say He was John the Baptist, some say He was Elijah, and others thought He was just one of the prophets. Although they were all His disciples, at that moment, only Peter had the proper understanding of who Christ was when He asked them, "Who do you say I am?" While they have spent many months living with and listening to Him, the view of others clouded their perspective of Him. Amidst the misconceptions, only Peter understood that Jesus was the Messiah they had waited for.

To remain grounded, we need to constantly remember that we are saved by the grace of God. As believers, we are part of a privileged group of people who are called to live like Christ, loving the world He died for but hating the sin in it. Our constant response to anyone walking outside the confines of the Bible should be genuine compassion and not smirk. Instead of debating how far the world is walking away from God, we can develop the habit of living out the faith we so jealously guard. Our salvation cost God the death of His dear son, but we have a responsibility to work it out daily in trembling and fear (Philippians 2:12).

SOMETHING ABOUT GOD'S PRESENCE

"You make known to me the path of life; you will fill me with joy in your presence, with eternal pleasures at your right hand." Psalm 16:11

There is just nothing like God's presence. In Exodus 33, God told Moses to lead the Israelites to the promised land without Him. He told Moses that although He would not go with them, the land would be flowing with milk and honey and that He would send His angels ahead of them. Despite the promises, Moses refused to lead the Israelites into the land until God said in verse 14, *"My Presence will go with you, and I will give you rest."* He understood that without God's presence, they were just like any other tribe. He knew no amount of prosperity could replace God's presence because His presence is greater than all the angels of Heaven.

The peace that comes from God's presence is unmatchable, and no wealth, health, or fame can be a substitute for it. Dwelling in God's presence renews our strength for all battles. It sets our mind on Him and eases the burden off our shoulders for Christ to handle.

Starting each day in His presence renews my strength for the journey. It makes me see Him in the rays of light that break through the dawn when I wake in the morning and the cloud that blankets the sky as I sleep at night. His presence calms my fears and gives me wings to fly above all adversities. I can say without doubt that walking with God alone is better than having all the world's armies behind me. He is constant, merciful, and gracious.

Understanding the power of God's presence allows us to subdue the overwhelming tug-of-war we experience daily. His presence floods our minds with an ocean of joy that can only come from knowing that the creator of heaven and earth is on our side. It reminds us that we are never alone and that the God of the universe stands right by us as we go through the dark tunnels of life and stand on lighted mountaintops.

THE RUSTLE OF THE WIND

"The wind blows wherever it pleases. You hear its sound, but you cannot tell where it comes from or where it is going..." John 3:8a

I woke up to a loud whizzing sound outside my window. It was so loud and constant that I thought there must be more to it than just air, so I opened the window to see. As soon as I lifted the window, I was welcomed by a gush of strong breeze that lifted the curtains. Yes, it was the wind, the invisible companion of humanity and the proof of life for every living thing. Until you take that last gasp of it, you are welcomed among the living. The wind is everywhere, yet it is only seen when it forms a destructive tornado or moves the sea in a hurricane.

As I pulled the window back down that early morning, I could not help but marvel at the strength of something I could only feel through my skin, giving me chills. I could hear the shingles rustle but could not touch the air. I sat on the edge of my bed and thought of the presence of God and the fact that though we cannot see Him, He is sovereign over all things that pertain to life.

When the people of Athens worshipped on an altar with the inscription "The unknown God," Paul called out their ignorance in Acts 17:22-28. Although one might think that it was enough for them to acknowledge the existence of God, God does not need any man's approval. He cannot be contained in an altar made by man's hands, and His sovereignty speaks through everything that has life. He shaped the sphere of humanity through His outstretched arms by creating all things.

Like the gentle breeze that blows softly on a delicate rosebud or the raging one that pulls a giant tree from its foundation and scatters the sea, we might not be able to touch God, but He is always present in all things and at all times. He is more than the force behind creation or a mysterious being watching from a faraway galaxy. He exists in every detail of the fabric of the universe. He is Yahweh, powerful, immortal, invisible, invincible, sovereign over all things, and Almighty.

Our doubt of the existence of God cannot erase Him nor reduce a pinch from all He is. However, our acknowledgment of God, through the acceptance of redemption by Christ, expands our horizons beyond human comprehension. We might be unable to touch God, but we see Him in the firmament, the deep ends of the earth's oceans, and the complex wonder of a tiny anthill. He is not an elusive father, for in Him we live, move, and have our being (Acts 17:28).

BEFORE YOU THROW THE NEXT STONE

"He saved us, not because of righteous things we had done, but because of his mercy. He saved us through the washing of rebirth and renewal by the Holy Spirit." Titus 3:5

In this tech age of living behind our computer screens, we have grown accustomed to taking the judgment throne of our self-designed castles to condemn others. We live like hunters looking for the next prey to fall into our bucket of "the unforgivable." The moment we hear someone somewhere is caught on camera doing something wrong, we scramble for our justice wand and banish them from the circle of "the perfect people."

Although we sing the song "Amazing grace, how sweet the sound that saved a wretch like me," we often forget how helpless we are outside of God's grace. When we join in the chants to destroy other people because they make mistakes, we diminish the cost of our salvation. We neglect the power

222

of the grace that saved us through faith, obedience, mercy and hope in Christ Jesus. Our righteous pride makes us set ourselves higher than the mortal beings we are, thinking we are gods and judges over people. Nevertheless, without Christ, we are as broken and full of errors as any criminal.

While I hold the right to protect myself from guilt-trippers, I constantly remind myself of my limitations and caution my haughty heart to humble itself before the throne of grace. I want to be like Christ, to love as He loved, and to see people how He sees them. I want to extend forgiveness from my heart before I condemn and offer repentance before I give up on people. I want to look inward all the time to acknowledge that I am all that I am by the continuous work of the Holy Spirit and that I can do nothing right except through God's grace.

When the people who brought the adulteress to Jesus in John 8 asked that He join in their chants to condemn her, He said, *"Let any one of you who is without sin be the first to throw a stone at her."* Verse 7b. It is so refreshing to see Christ's love in action. One would expect that His focus would be on the woman's sin and disgrace, repulsed by the deed and rebuking her for it. Instead, Jesus was more tuned in to the possibilities of who she could become when she received His forgiveness. The men eager to condemn her left ashamed because the moment they looked inward, they knew they were not better than her.

Before you cast the next stone or label the next social media victim, you might want to remember what Jesus said.

We are products of grace; the only difference between us and that "terrible person" is Christ. Like the scene in the temple courts in John 8, Jesus stands between us and the people we are so eager to condemn. Our response must always acknowledge Him, sitting there, writing in the sands of our life, telling us not to be so prompt to pull others down but to call them to "go and sin no more."

THE QUIET WHISPERS

"Looking unto Jesus the author and finisher of our faith; who for the joy that was set before him endured the cross, despising the shame, and is set down at the right hand of the throne of God." Hebrews 12:2

In a world as busy and unpredictable as ours, it is easy for us to lose focus and be pulled from different sides as we are driven by different daily demands for survival. A typical day for anyone is downright hectic and, most of the time, exhausting; now, think of a man or a woman who has to work multiple jobs to keep their life together.

Our eyes constantly shift from one direction to another, and sometimes, even our sleep eludes us because we are convinced we did not get enough done to secure a restful tomorrow. Our hearts are heavy with desires and hopes to reach a place of peace and quiet eventually. Finding time to focus is a daily struggle, and we forget to weigh the importance of drawing strength from the One who gives us breath and creates us for His glory.

Surrounded by so much noise, we fail to hear those quiet whispers of God, telling us to find rest and keep our gaze on Him. If we keep looking heavenward, no matter what pulls and shoves us here on earth, we are sure His grace is sufficient for us. When Peter saw Jesus walking on water in the book of Mathew 14:25-31 and asked to join Him, his eyes were on Jesus. As long as he kept those eyes on Christ, he stayed afloat, but the moment he shifted his gaze from Jesus and looked at the water, he began to sink.

One thing is for sure: our answer is not in the raging waters around us, so we need to keep our eyes up to hear the quiet whispers from Heaven. Mathew 6:22 states that *"the light of the body is the eye: If therefore thine eye be single, thy whole body shall be full of light."* Take a minute to try looking up with one eye and on the ground with the other. It is impossible because you can only look up or down at the same time. So, keep those eyes on Jesus, and you will stay afloat despite everything trying to drown you.

God is constant, and as we continue to trust and listen to Him, we will experience the calmness that washes over the soul of everyone who looks to Jesus. Regardless of the uncertainties around us, hope, peace, assurance, and abounding grace flow from Heaven to us when Christ is our focus. We are constantly reminded in Psalms 24:1 that *"The earth is the LORD'S and the fullness thereof; the world and they that dwell therein."* When we fully understand who God is, the reality of His sovereignty will govern our lives, and the constant assurance of His presence will keep us going. Look beyond the stress, the unpaid bills, the pain, the disappointment, and the uncertainties that are swallowing you up, and allow the peace of God to rule your life.

"Come unto me, all ye that labor and are heavy laden, and I will give you rest." Mathew 11:28.

THE KING, THE BABY, AND THE MANGER

"But God hath chosen the foolish things of the world to confound the wise; and God hath chosen the weak things of the world to confound the things which are mighty;" 1 Corinthians 1:27

Comprehending the story of the birth of Jesus can overwhelm our human minds. It is hard to fathom why the creator of the world would leave His throne to be born as a vulnerable little baby just to save His creations. Although He made everything, He still laid them all down to walk the path of humanity.

The culmination of Christ's birth envelopes the best love story ever written. God chose to come through the most unlikely woman in the most unlikely town and among the most unlikely creatures. His mother, Mary, was a young virgin (Luke 1:27). His birthplace was Bethlehem, a town so small that it was not one of the major tribes of Israel. Micah 5:2 states, *"But as for you, Bethlehem Ephrathah, too little to be among the clans of Judah...*" Because there was no room in any inn, the King of the universe was born in a manger among animals (Luke 2:7).

The birth of Christ is the greatest occurrence in human history. An unworthy world welcomed the purest being to pass through its core, yet His first visitors were lowly shepherds. He did not have a red carpet sprawled before Him, nor the world's nobles lined up to affirm Him. He left an eternal kingdom to dwell in a temporary world and abandoned the worship of Cherubs for the shouts of "crucify Him."

The Christmas story is the story of the King of kings leaving His throne on high to be conceived by a young virgin, hunted by a jealous ruler, born in a manger, lived perfectly as a common man, and unjustly crucified by His creations. While this might not be the most picture-perfect story or measure up to our definition of a hero's welcome and exit, it is written in the language of love and the blood of Christ. It is good news, the birth of hope and joy, and the rescue of man from sin and eternal death. Announcing His birth, the angels said to the shepherds in Luke 2:10, *"Do not be afraid. I bring you good news that will cause great joy for all the people. Today in the town of David, a Savior has been born to you; He is the Messiah, the Lord."*

We might not fully understand why the season of Christ's birth shines a bright light on the world each year, regardless of everything coming against us; however, we know what the season represents. It is much more than the brightest light or the whitest snowfall. It serves as a reminder of God's sacrifice for us to be reunited with Him and the depth of His love for humankind.

WISDOM COMES ONLY FROM GOD'S WORD

"The entrance of Your words gives light;
It gives understanding to the simple." Psalm 119:130

Martin Luther was one of the most influential people of his time and a great force of influence on the basic tenets of our Christian faith. When he decided to drop out of college to become a Monk, he did so out of fear of death because of a thunderstorm encounter. However, his continuous study of the Bible transformed his understanding enough to challenge the status quo and the whole church order. God's word opened his eyes to see beyond the dictates of men and for him to fall in love with who God is and not what men defined Him to be.

God's word is enough to lead, guide, teach, uphold, and sustain us as we journey through life. The Bible is not just words and letters written in the dusty book on our dressing tables or the polished ones we only pick up on Sunday mornings. God's word is light; it is alive and true! As dark and confusing as navigating the world is, full illumination comes from learning the scriptures. Psalms 119:105 says, *"Your word is a lamp.... And a light."*

As followers of Christ, if we do not live by the word, we will look like the world. Our path is only lighted by God's word and should serve as the single channel through which all our thoughts and conclusions are filtered. What good to a hungry man is a meal prepared by the best chef if he does not eat it? No matter how delicious it smells or looks, there is zero nutritional value until the food is swallowed. Tasting is not enough because it simply fuels the hunger and desire to eat.

I search Google for everything, from trending hairstyles to the best ointment for a bug bite. However, I know I must stick to the authenticity of God's word regarding things that pertain to life and godliness. Before we ask Google or look for the answer on YouTube, maybe we should develop the habit of searching from the most enduring and reliable source of information in the world—the Bible. God's word is the greatest treasure anyone can find and has stood the test of time. It's been burned and banned, and many people are still dying because they own it.

When we live by the word, we are changed both within and without, and we become who God wants us to be, not perfect through our works but perfect through His continuous workings in us. Hebrews 4:12 says, *"For the word of God is quick, and powerful, and sharper than any two-edged sword, piercing even to the dividing asunder of soul and spirit, and of the joints and marrow, and is a discerner of the thoughts and intents of the heart."*

Ours is a privileged generation because we have unlimited access to God's word, including the life of Christ, from which to learn. What more do we need to be fearless and shine as bright as Jesus did when He charted this same earth course? While physical open pages are my favorite, there are other ways to access the Bible now, giving us options to read or listen to it.

I have been asking myself these questions and will continue to do so; "What will this situation look like if I look at it through the lens of God's word?"; "How will I respond to this man/woman if I see them through the examples in God's word?"; Where will I stand on issues around me if I take time to sift through them through God's word?": "What will my life look like daily if I live based on God's word?"

Following Jesus is a lifelong adventure, and walking with other Christians brings Heaven closer! Sharing life with Christian friends is crucial for growth and sustainability.

City Church Life Group (Send Forth, Florida, 2017)

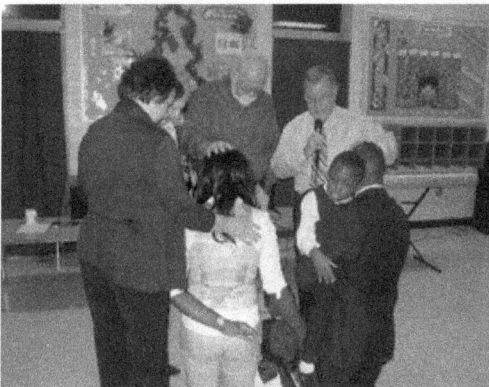

Christian Heritage Church (CHC) Pastors Ron McCants and Don Jackson (Florida, 2012)

"Go Ye" Church Choir (Lagos, 1993)

Word of Faith Bible Institute (WOFBI) (Graduation, Lagos, 2003)

Winners Chapel NYSC Choir (Yobe, 2001)

Northview Church Life Group, (Indiana, 2024)

Joshua's Journey with Pastor Ron and Ms. Barbara McCants (Florida, 2011)

NYSC "The Family" (Yobe, 2000)

Best Youth Award "Go Ye Church" with Apostle T.A Iyanda (Lagos, 1992); OND Graduation with Sarah and Jane (Ogun, 1996)

Grace Church Life Group (Indiana, 2018)

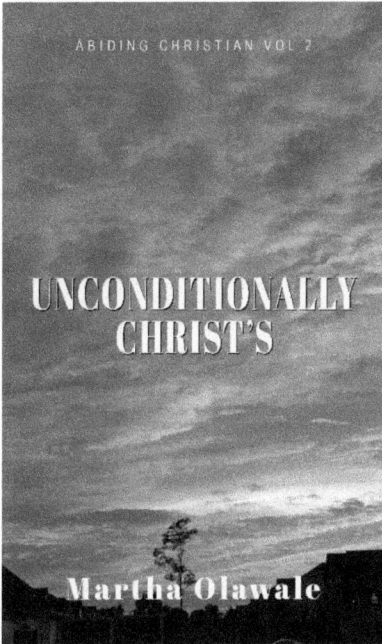

Being a Christian answers all the questions about who we are, how we respond to the world, and where we are going. Christianity is not a significant part of our identity; it encompasses our entire identity. The greatest gift anyone can receive is salvation in Jesus Christ. While our walk with Jesus does not level all the mountains we have to face in life, it helps to clear the fog so we know how to climb them. "Unconditionally Christ's" is the second volume of the Abiding Christian books. As Christians, we are assured of our Lord's commitment to us and the unwavering love of Jesus despite our shortcomings. This book will encourage you to grow in your walk with God and commitment to living like Jesus no matter what life throws at you.

www.ingramcontent.com/pod-product-compliance
Lightning Source LLC
LaVergne TN
LVHW091250080426
835510LV00007B/193